Bringing a Garden to Life

Bringing a Garden to Life

Carol Williams

Illustrations by Newton H. Stubbing

 BANTAM BOOKS
New York • Toronto • London • Sydney • Auckland

BRINGING A GARDEN TO LIFE
A Bantam Book/January 1998

Library of Congress Cataloging-in-Publication Data
Williams, Carol, 1948–
Bringing a garden to life / by Carol Williams.
p. cm.
Includes bibliographical references and index.
ISBN 0-553-09680-x
1. Gardening. 2. Gardening—Philosophy. I. Title.
SB453.W495 1998
635—dc21
97-28529
CIP

Published simultaneously in the United States and Canada

Bantam Books are published by Bantam Books, a division of Bantam Doubleday Dell Publishing Group, Inc. Its trademark, consisting of the words "Bantam Books" and the portrayal of a rooster, is Registered in U.S. Patent and Trademark Office and in other countries. Marca Registrada. Bantam Books, 1540 Broadway, New York, New York 10036.

Printed in the United States of America
BVG   10 9 8 7 6 5 4 3 2 1

For Eesha, Gabriel, and Kari
with love and thanks

O chestnut tree, great rooted blossomer,
Are you the leaf, the blossom or the bole?
O body swayed to music, O brightening glance,
How can we know the dancer from the dance?

William Butler Yeats, "Among School Children"

Contents

Bringing *a* Garden *to* Life

Introduction

This book is for people who love gardening and for those who I hope soon will. It is intended as a guide to making a garden and sustaining it as it grows and changes. The aim is to encourage, so the book tries for simplicity: no previous experience is necessary to follow these instructions. But while it may be simple, it suggests no shortcuts to a quick result, because here no result is more desired than the enjoyment of the work at hand.

"Things won are done; joy's soul lies in the doing," wrote Shakespeare, who must have known. This is true of all of life, but, in my experience, nowhere more transparently than in the garden, where the gardener's activity joins with that of seeds that sprout, buds unfolding, green wood turning to brown.

I do not propose any particular way a garden ought to be, only describe the everyday jobs that gradually bring about the conditions in which a happy community of flowers, herbs, vegetables, and trees, and the insects, birds, animals, and people that belong with them, can thrive. The first part of this book concerns thinking about the garden as a place and laying it out, then preparing and cultivating the soil, planting and transplanting, weeding and pruning. The second part considers how these activities apply to the different sorts of garden plants—the flowers, vegetables, herbs, and trees, and the various ways they can be approached. The final chapter is about tools and about time, the context in which all garden work is done.

I am quite sure that gardeners who follow, each in their own ways, this outline for working unhurriedly in their gardens will eventually create gardens of a variety and loveliness that I could never imagine. But I hope that they will also be encouraged to find interest and beauty where it is not usually expected—in the raw, early stages of beginning as much as in mellow maturity; in a neglected garden in need of reclamation as much as in an impeccably clipped and tidy one; even in the mornings after a big storm when all plans seem wrecked and one needs to begin again. In the garden, every season and situation carries the seeds of the next; in the everyday tasks of gardening one comes to see them.

Gardening—like frying eggs or driving nails—used to be learned half-consciously at home, simply by watching. In this kind of learning one picks up not just the details and texture of the craft—the proper sizzle of the butter in the pan before one breaks the egg, the angle at which one sets a foot on a spade—but also the disposition of the person doing it. If there is urgency and zest, this is probably what caught one's attention to begin with, and they too are learned. I was lucky in that way. My mother loved to garden; her happy snipping and tying, watering and digging formed the background of my childhood. Then, while still young and impressionable, I married an orchardist with a sympathetic touch toward all plants. Watching his sure hands in orchard and garden furthered my education.

As a garden writer for the local newspaper, I learned from conversations with readers that this kind of transmission is becoming rarer. People move in and out of places where there are no gardens, or they have gardens but have moved far away from the relatives and neighbors who might have been their mentors. Because of this gap, I have made an effort to pass on the small things one might notice, sometimes out of the corner of an eye, when following along behind a gardening friend who is intent on the job. For me, and I believe for many others, these are what have made the difference, opened doors. I hope I can convey the sense of this to new gardeners, and that experienced ones will not be bored but reminded and reinspired.

The golden rule of gardening is to pay attention to local conditions of weather and soil. It is difficult to discuss in general terms what is by nature specific and idiosyncratic. I have tried here to show how each garden task relates to the fundamental principles of enlivening soil and growing plants, but also to make it clear that these processes, and consequently the jobs that go with them, must happen on a different schedule in different places. (Everyone needs good regional advice and chronology, so a list of more localized sources appears in the Readings and Resources section at the end, as well as suggestions in the text for when it is best to consult one's neighbors.)

Now and again I use a particular garden—my own or someone else's—as a point of reference, so as not to become lost in too much abstraction. Most of these gardens are on eastern Long Island, which has some sandy soil, some rich loam, and four distinct seasons, each tempered by the nearby Atlantic Ocean. Conditions will be quite different for gardeners in Montana or Georgia. But I hope it is clear throughout where the "rule" to be followed is to act in accordance with what is actually going on, not to do exactly what I do. Gardeners need above all to use all five senses, often six, and to have the courage to try things out. Ultimately, the surest way to learn the best planting date for corn, the flowering times of lilac, is to watch carefully in one's own garden.

When I mention my garden in this book, readers should not imagine anything especially impressive. It is the backyard of the first house my then husband and I could afford to buy, where I still live seventeen years later. In one way it cannot help but be lovely; it borders on a tidal creek and overlooks the sea. On the other hand, it has taken great efforts merely to establish that there is a garden there at all. A busy road runs along one edge, there is a school bus garage on one side and a boatyard on the other, from all of which issue sudden roars of motors and occasional billows of smoke. And though I have had time to bring the garden to a certain sweet maturity—fruit trees that bear and lean toward us, daffodils that dance all the way to the pond, a swing that two out of three children have outgrown—there have also been hurricanes, floods, family crises, and deer depredations, each of which has on occasion brought the garden almost back to the original desolation in which I found it.

All these troubles allow me to say that the limitations of the garden and the obstacles to its progress have been no handicap to the enjoyment it has brought me; perhaps they have even increased it. It is known that people who are ill have regained health in the garden; broken hearts have been made whole. But I think it is not the garden so much as the gardening that performs these miracles.

Some years ago a friend of mine, a skilled and inspired gardener, fell prey to one of those sudden and paralyzing black depressions that sometimes attack in the middle of life. I went to visit, found him huddled on a couch, but was pleased to find that even in the depths he could still muster some wry humor. The onset of despair had, he said, coincided with the publication of several pages of photographs of his garden in vivid color in a glossy magazine. "When I saw these pictures," he said, as we leafed through those images of perfection, "I felt the garden was finished, all over." Though he smiled, it was not altogether a joke. When something that is alive stands still, becoming a thing to be admired, danger lurks. (He has since recovered and gone back to the garden, where I recently saw him nursing seedling trees.)

A hundred years ago, in introducing his *Manual of Gardening,* Liberty Bailey, the great American horticulturalist, wrote that "every decade needs its own manual of handicraft." He was partly joking, partly serious, for he knew that times change and so do the aspirations of those who live in them. Certainly in this past decade, as the millennium approaches, more and more people are involving themselves closely with their gardens. Social critics see this trend as an escape from the crises and complexities of modern life, and cynical marketers view it as yet another greed to pander to—the garden as a room to furnish as expensively as possible. But I think that this critique seriously misreads the mood of the time.

This "manual" was written in the belief that today more than ever the impulse to garden represents the opposite of those things. People are turning to their gardens not to consume but to actively create, not to escape from reality but to observe it closely. In doing this they experience the connectedness of creation and the profoundest sources of being. That the world we live in and the activity of making it are one seamless whole is something that we may occasionally glimpse. In the garden, we know.

Chapter 1 Making a Place

O Lady! we receive but what we give,
And in our lives alone does Nature live.

Samuel Taylor Coleridge, "Dejection: An Ode"

If the Garden has been properly laid out, there need not be a maze
in it. For the quest, the puzzlement, the contingency of the place of
rest with its bench and rosebushes in the center of it all, the ease of
entrance and its welcoming entrapment, the problems of homing,
will all have been provided by the Garden itself. And the maze's
parable, unrolling beneath the hurrying feet of the last wanderers
on a summer evening that now chills and darkens—the parable of
how there can be no clarity of truth without puzzlement, no joy
without losing one's way—will be propounded by the Garden's
final perfection, namely that in it is no trace of the designer, that
no image of him can ever be found. He—you—will have disappeared into the ground of the place that has been made.

John Hollander, *Instructions to the Landscaper*

Adam and Eve were born in a garden, and gardens
are still where people go to renew themselves by meeting creation. In that encounter gardeners have a particular advantage,
because they see much more than meets the ordinary eye. The
garden that is hedged, fountained, sheltered by ancient trees may
take many years to realize, but I am in a garden as soon as I pick up
my hoe. The garden one meets when one participates in its making is vivid and alive, and casts a sweet green shade of its own.

The distinction between those two gardens, the finished one and the one being made, is seldom clear-cut. Sometimes this leads to confusion and the confusion to discontent. Ten years ago I had a job writing a gardening column in the local newspaper. I never had trouble thinking what to write about, just happily recorded the changes in the season as they came and the tasks in my garden that went with them. Now I see that because I so much enjoyed that emerging garden, the columns gave the impression that I was onto something worth having. The difficulty came when the readers wanted to see what it was.

Acquaintances I ran into at the post office began to ask if they could come and see my garden. "It must be wonderful!" "Oh, it is," I would agree and invite them over. Some of these visits were a success; two even led to lasting friendships. The visitors and I would wave our arms over almost-empty beds declaiming about the flowers and vegetables that would fill them one day, admire the compost pile, the microscopic seedlings that had at last come up at the site of the future rock garden, the young home orchard. Then they would hurry home to get on with their gardens and I would go back to mine.

But more often, the encounters were discordant and bewildering, and sometimes I felt I was losing my grip on the garden I loved. I would begin by pointing out the mixed hedgerow of holly, hazel, cedar, and lilac, the Gardiner's Island peach tree (which produces delicious white-fleshed peaches with skins that are shriveled and green) that grew from a pit, the glacial rock overhung by the exquisite, pale yellow, honey-scented native azalea. But soon I would hear my explaining voice trailing into lack of conviction, unnerved by the disappointment in my visitors' eyes. Through their perplexity I began to see another garden: undeniably present, but sparse, incomplete, and littered with the equipment of everyday life: pajamas on the clothesline, rusty tractor parts dwarfing the rock-and-azalea configuration, trucks and cars rumbling and flashing through the gaps between the knee-high hedgerow plantings. The young apple trees—mere whips, never very visible in the gray spring air—could, in a certain light, disappear altogether.

The visitors and I would part, embarrassed. Had I deluded them, or perhaps myself? Was the wonderful garden something I had only imagined? I would make dejected efforts to move a tricycle, cut the grass. Or I would go listlessly indoors, unable to face so much emptiness. Then a little time would pass, perhaps one night. In the morning a small red bud would appear on a gray, thorny rose stump, or some thyme seeds sprout, primroses open. Before my eyes the garden burgeoned again—green, compelling, no fantasy at all. And I would go to work in it.

Over the years, the garden in my imagination and the one outside the kitchen windows have drawn closer together. Now the buds on the narrow apple whips are branches loaded with fruit. People bump their heads on them. Boundaries are defined, no more gaps in the hedge: birds nest there and children hide, and the road seems far away, even though it is not. The flower beds are thick with peony, phlox, lavender, bees. The backhoe is gone, so the rock and azalea are sculpted against sky and distant water. There is a gate, and anyone who passes through knows they have arrived, where once they might not have been quite sure.

Though all this brings great pleasure, I do remember that to me, the gardener, the fragile early garden—partly tangible, part imagined—was as satisfying as this present substantial one. Imagination is not fantasy, but active interest. "I feel," wrote William Blake, "that a Man can be happy in This World. And I know that This World Is a World of Imagination and Vision. . . . The tree which moves some to tears of joy is in the eyes of others only a Green thing which stands in the way." Gardeners step into this world of imagination as soon as they begin to garden. They cannot plant a dry seed without awareness of the flame of life inside it, or prune a bare branch without sensing clustered blossoms and leaves.

Following the earth

No two of the gardens I have visited and loved have been alike. They have been formal and austere or wild and abundant, rural and expansive or tiny and pristine. But each has evoked, through but beyond the personality of the gardener who made it, a distillation of its place on the earth. This is why I cannot bring myself to say, as some books do, "Before picking up your spade take out graph paper and ruler and plan your garden." Or, "Study photographs of gardens you admire and reproduce them where you live." The danger is that in starting with a picture of what should be, a gardener may lose sight of what is. A great garden says, "*This* is where you are." It is as though the gardener's work was not so much to impose as to make visible, by artistry, something already there in the rocks, trees, and breezes of that locality, the spirit under the ground and in the air.

I think all gardeners keep this idea somewhere in their minds, but the Taoist gardeners and garden poets of ancient China took it as their essential calling. Their gardens, whether vast palace grounds or tiny plots outside hermits' huts, were intended as revelations of the flow of *chi* or life spirit as it manifested in a particular place. According to the accounts of travelers in ancient China, not only gardens but a cultivated rural landscape of surpassing beauty arose from this consciousness.

It was among contemplative Taoist monks at least two thousand years ago that the art or science of *feng shui,* or geomancy, originated. Certain monks became adept at determining the flow of chi on any site. As dowsers look for water, the feng shui masters charted the sources and sinks of spiritual energy in a given place and thereby uncovered its essential genius. To this day the Chinese of Taiwan and Hong Kong (perhaps covertly also on the mainland) call in a feng shui master before embarking on work at any building site or garden. Sometimes this process is crudely conceived as a matter of good or bad luck—get it wrong and your company stock will fall, get it right and you prosper. But it originates in the more subtle and profound recognition that the places in which one feels truly well—close to God, restored to oneself—are those made in harmony with the spirit of earth and cosmos. In the sixth century BCE, Lao Tzu wrote in his book of the Way (*Tao Te Ching*):

> Man follows the earth
> The earth follows the universe
> The universe follows the Tao
> The Tao follows only itself.

Gardeners, I think, can become geomancers of their own gardens when they work in them with love and imagination. They notice how the soil is; they follow the course of water, where it puddles, where it flows; they plant a little of this and a little of that, discover what fails, what thrives, and how and where a plant turns toward the sun. Gardeners are also geomancers when they put down their hoes and find the places where they love to linger and where they are inspired to move on, where and when light filters through flower petals, where the cold winds come from, where the sunny shelters are, where the comforting shade, where birds nest. From a thousand homely parts a picture slowly arises that becomes more than their sum.

This kind of knowledge takes time to acquire. While it is accumulating, gardeners endure (or perhaps enjoy, depending on their temperaments) a certain amount of tenuousness and lack of form. The garden may not "look like anything" even while there is much for the imagination to see. But I do not think there is a better way to ensure that when the garden does take shape, its forms, hues, and scents will be rooted in the place where it is.

The garden map

Working without a fixed plan does not mean beginning with nothing. Gardeners require several essential tools for starting. One, as has already been suggested, is a "map" or inventory of what is there.

A garden map is only as good as it is complete. If one is going to make a garden on a site where the house has not yet been built, the map must be made early and studied with particular care for much is at stake and there may not be much time before the builders arrive. Christopher Alexander, in *A Pattern Language,* his classic book of design archetypes, offers the essential advice for this stage:

> Buildings must always be placed on those parts of the land which are in the worst condition not the best. . . . On no account place buildings in the places which are most beautiful. In fact do the opposite. . . . Leave those areas that are the most precious, beautiful, comfortable and healthy as they are, and build new structures in those parts of the site which are least pleasant now.

It happens too often that a site is chosen because of some lovely aspect, which is then destroyed in building the house. A southern slope, grove of trees, grassy knoll—these are gifts of fate. The house can be made beautiful by its builders. As the Chinese *Yuan Yeh* pointed out a thousand years ago, "It is easy to embellish the pillars and insert the beams but hard to get the *huai* tree to grow."

Often it is necessary to work closely with the builders, marking certain bushes and trees to make sure they will not be cut down to make way for the lumberyard truck. Near where I live, I have seen acre sites thick with shadbush, red cedar, and bayberry razed to make room for one little house. At the other extreme, when I visit my oldest son at his college in California, I come upon whole libraries and classroom buildings nestled in a redwood forest so gently that they look as though they had been lowered from the sky.

If it is too late, and the builders have cut down the huai tree or flattened the knoll, a map of what is left will still be all to the good. The trees that remain can be noted, and so can the spaces between them, the rocks, edges of buildings, areas where soil seems promising, those where it looks bad, and puddles, slopes, and prominences.

The relative proportions of sun and shade need to be carefully watched. They will determine the mood and content of the garden. I suppose it is possible to predict what will happen to the shifting patterns of light and shadow as the sun's angle and arc dip and rise throughout the year and as the leaves of the various trees open and shed, but the effects are so subtle and complex that I cannot quite believe it. It is much better to wait and see, delaying serious planning and planting till one has seen four seasons come and go.

Few gardeners could be happy with a garden entirely without shade, or one with no sun. In either case, something can always be done. But it needs careful watching. A garden with no shade is almost unthinkable, having no sense of shelter and oasis. Gardeners may want to plant trees at once, but should take time to think carefully about what *kind* of shadow they will throw. A willow will cast a light and dappled shade; a maple or chestnut a deep and heavy one. One must consider how early or late a tree will leaf out in spring or shed in fall, whether or not to choose an evergreen that will cast shade even in winter. Most of all thought must be given to *where* shade is wanted, for visual seclusion or a cool sitting place in summer, or for cooling the house itself, and where it is not: where one might grow vegetables, where the sun's warmth is welcome on cool mornings.

A garden with only shade, besides being melancholy, can be

frustrating for gardeners who like to grow a little of everything. Many lovely plants do well in the shade, especially with extra attention to the soil, but many more do not—no roses, no pumpkins. Most gardeners covet at least a small area of full sun. But caution is essential here. Rather than hastily cutting down a tree that may have taken thirty years to grow, it is worth investigating precisely when and from where the shadows really fall. Otherwise, one might cut the wrong tree, or a whole one when it might have been enough to take out a few branches.

In taking over a garden that already exists, it often takes four seasons just to discover what plants are there, and to begin to decide what to keep, what to transplant, what to give away or throw in the compost. The bare earth next to the shed in March might be a bed of peonies in June. A bush may be a "green thing in the way" in August, but not when one has witnessed the crimson of its leaves in September or the drama of its winter branches. Gardeners know what a blessing it is to find trees and shrubs that have already made themselves at home, shaped by the prevailing rocks and winds, or the delight of flowers gone wild, a lawn full of violets, a sudden burst of red poppies in June. A woman I know bought her house only because of the thirty-foot pear tree in its tiny garden and has never been sorry.

On the other hand, planting that has been done mindlessly—dour yews lined up across a lawn, a volunteer maple that blocks the sun—can actually make a place much less than it is, and gardeners do not need to feel disrespectful if they pull it out. Nor can they assume that established beds are necessarily in the best places. Perhaps they were, when they were dug, but now are overshadowed; or maybe the previous occupant made a mistake.

Many aspects of the garden cannot be drawn on a map—sweet sounds, wind in the trees, all sorts of scents. But they still need somehow to be inventoried, so they do not escape the attention but become part of the conscious forming of the garden. Writing brief garden poems is an aid to noticing what one notices. It is worth trying, even if one has never written poetry before. These are not for publication, but strictly to put in the garden notebook along with records of first and last frosts and the flowering times of lilac. It helps to study the great exemplars: Li Po, Basho, and Keats all offer economy of form and sharpness of sense. This is Shiki:

> After a shower
> the clearing sky smells faintly
> of hawthorne blossoms.

Fences, hedges, and edges

Setting boundaries, like making maps, helps a gardener see what the garden might be. But while a map can remain on paper or in careful observations in the gardener's mind, boundaries must be drawn clearly on the ground. Edges focus the attention. A garden can leap into existence simply by being encircled.

At college I took a botany class in which each student was given for a term her own quadrant in the woods—a section of forest, fifteen feet on each side, marked off by a piece of string, in which to make observations. I became very attached to my quadrant and often revisited it. The piece of string became my door into the forest: within I saw lichens and moss, oak leaves unfolding, blueberries flowering, arbutus trailing. Without it I was simply "in the woods." So it is in a garden. Without a boundary a garden can blow away, dissipate. Everything within the boundary becomes significant, enhanced.

Whether a garden's edge needs to be a piece of string, a rose hedge, or a ten-foot wall depends on what is on the other side. A busy road sucks up all fragrance and birdsong in its dust, roar, and gasoline fumes. Therefore a garden beside a road needs a wall or substantial hedge. If the garden adjoins other lovely gardens, faces a view of fields or distant mountains, the boundary can be much softer, more permeable—vines on a light trellis, flowering shrubs, or high-branching trees. "If beautiful views are what one wants, one makes good use of the groups of trees" says the *Yuan Yeh*. One end of my long narrow garden abuts the noisy, dangerous highway, the other meets the tidal creek opening to the sea. So one end is bounded by a mixed hedge twenty feet thick, the other by the glimmer of the horizon.

I think that in every gardener's soul there is necessarily both a longing for boundary and also a kind of aversion. I grew up in England, where garden walls are considered only polite, and live now in an American community where they are illegal. I could laugh at this paradox if I did not also feel it in myself. English hedges and walls protect not plants so much as the solitude of the gardeners, their right to look inward. The wide-open landscapes of New England country towns and suburbs are symbols of longed-for community and reunion with nature.

The identification of boundaries with property lines is one probable cause of antipathy. There is something ugly about a fence that seems to exist only to keep others out. But insofar as a garden, especially a small one, must have a boundary—almost a skin—in order to exist at all, that boundary expresses something else. A wall with flowers in its chinks, a fence through which phlox and daisies escape onto the roadside, glimpses of flowering branches, bamboo, a welcoming gate—these kinds of membranes send a different message, one that might be grasped with equanimity from either side.

There are other appropriate boundaries besides those of property. On a short, narrow block in Manhattan the occupants decided that the limits of their individual backyards were too confined to make sense as places. Therefore they gave up their tiny separate yards in favor of one (still not very big) garden that all share. The boundaries are now the surrounding ten houses, and, at least for the time being, a true walled garden thrives at the center of one of the world's great and supposedly harshest cities.

Seclusion in the garden

Sometimes boundaries need to be drawn within a garden as well as, or instead of, at its perimeter. One reason might be to create secluded places from which to watch the garden unobserved. Children find such spaces very quickly, taking over the hollow tree, the green bush with a hiding place among its trunks, as soon as they arrive. Once inside, they look out, watch a robin drag out its worm, the light change, or the leaves fall. Adults need such places too.

If the garden does not already possess a bower, one can be made. Twenty years ago, I had a garden that was half of a tiny village yard shared with our landlord. He and I were very discreet, kept to our own sides, gardening with our backs to one another. (We actually invited each other over once a month to "see" each other's gardens, thereby acknowledging another sort of boundary, that of politely pretending not to look.) I loved that garden, but found that I never sat down in it; instead I kept ceaselessly at work, assiduously tending my plant experiments. I never quite knew why this was. Then one day my husband planted a *Viburnum carlesii*—six feet tall, fragrant, and very leafy—at an angle to the wall such that if I set my chair between wall and shrub, I would be completely hidden from view. This small niche changed my whole experience of the garden: from one in which I was

always active to one where I could sit and watch. The ninety-five plant experiments cohered and spoke, and the garden really began.

These quiet spots can become places in themselves, sometimes the very heart of a garden. They can remain unornamented—just a simple seat beside a bush, wall, or lattice screen. Or they can gradually develop, with perhaps some flat stones underfoot with scented thyme between them, or a small bed nearby planted with a few well-loved plants—one or two for each season. (*Viburnum carlesii* smells sweet in April, *rugosa* roses, especially one called Blanc Double de Courbet, for most of the summer.)

What the sitting place is made of matters less than where it is. The site must be located properly. Is it sunny in winter, shady in summer? Does it offer shelter from cold winds? The right glimpse of sky or tree? To find one's place, it is better not to be encumbered too soon with a heavy bench. The search will go better with something light to sit on—an old kitchen chair, or a canvas beach one—that can easily be moved around and placed as mood or light suggests. After some months, the spot to which one most often gravitates will make itself known, and that will be the place to plant the bench.

Between cultivated and wild

Another kind of boundary within a garden is that between the parts that are cultivated and those that are wild, woods perhaps, or meadow. In the garden I have now—outside the village and much bigger than the one with the viburnum—an area a hundred feet or so behind the house is carefully cultivated, every plant chosen and cared for. I prune the fruit trees, weed the beds, and cut the grass.

The region farther away is still "the garden" but is not much touched. Two or three times a year I hire a man with a reel mower to prevent it from being overgrown with briers. It is essentially a small meadow (sometimes tidal as the creek ebbs and flows with the equinoxes) under tall trees with a few bushes pruned mostly by wind and animals. Except for a path through it down to the creek, this part is left to grasses, wildflowers (cinquefoil, arrow-head violet, chicory), children's hide-and-seek games, screech owls, foxes, and the occasional inundation during big storms at high tides.

For years I did not think much about this division. It just happened. I could get to only a certain amount of garden work, and my cultivated areas gradually tapered away into those belonging to the deer and storms. But lately, because the deer have got too many and ravaged the plants near the house, I have had to build a fence and draw the line.

I resisted the fence for as long as I could and still wish I could do without seven feet of nylon mesh nailed onto cedar trunks, "invisible" though it is supposed to be. Yet, in a way I did not anticipate, being forced to acknowledge the difference has sharpened my apprehension of both the loveliness and delicacy within the fence and the wilderness and mystery without. Both parts of the garden seem more themselves, more distinctly present. Even if I could return to the Edenic years when the deer kept to their places and I did not need a fence, I would still look for a way—a few pickets, or a low hedge—to emphasize and mark the difference, and a gate through which to go back and forth.

Boundaries of use

How sociable the garden was.
We ate and talked in given light.
The children put their toys to grass
All the warm wakeful August night.

Thom Gunn, "Last Days at Teddington"

Other boundaries that shape the garden grow out of the choices gardeners make about which of life's activities to invite into the garden and which to leave out. Anyone lucky enough to have the use of a small piece of outside space in this crowded world is likely to find themselves wondering if they might want to dry their washing there, cook dinner, give children room to play, keep chickens, wash the car. Sooner or later gardeners have to decide if they are going to separate these activities off in a divided space— as in "yard" and "garden"—eliminate them from their lives, or make them part of the garden.

Gardens that are very carefully shaped, with clipped shrubs and hedges, and pathways opening onto sudden vistas or solemn urns, lose their drama and mystery if they become cluttered and quo-tidian. I know and admire several gardens like that. Some are the work of gardeners who are also painters or sculptors; some of gar-deners with a strong eye and controlling hand. Either way, the impulse is to create gardens that are removed from ordinary expe-rience. Like works of art, such gardens have the power to jolt vis-itors into another reality, of nature still, but also of association and dream.

In order to create such places, gardeners keep their grounds free of distraction. Some learn to be very tidy and put away their wheelbarrows, barbecues, and beach towels in sheds or discreet side yards. Or some lead austere and simple lives and dispense with such paraphernalia altogether. Sometimes, I suppose, this comes naturally; other times it is a conscious sacrifice.

I also know gardens where woodpiles, washing lines, children's games, and fireplaces are consciously integrated with peonies, roses, fruit trees, terraces. These gardens are also full of atmosphere and evocative power, but of a different sort. The woodpile makes a rustic fence; striped socks wave cheerfully from carved clothes posts, chickens cluck happily in their vine-covered henhouse. These gardens too can be beautiful and moving. When the tools and vestiges of everyday life are treated as lovingly as the roses and hedges, ordinary life is no longer so ordinary.

The only element of everyday life that I have never seen successfully integrated into a garden is the car. It might be the metal, the danger, or just the idea of going somewhere else, but a car parked in a small garden can make the garden almost disappear, and even a big garden loses much of its peaceful nature if cars can rush in and out at any moment. Many gardeners need cars, but it is always worth checking to see if more space than is strictly necessary is being given over to the driveway. Could the driveway be moved to one side and screened off with some shrubs or a fence? Sometimes it is possible to manage without a driveway and create a small parking area instead. Some of the serenest houses I know are approached on foot along leafy pathways.

Children in the garden

Gardeners who share their gardens with children usually have to abandon the pristine garden-set-apart approach. However, as soon as children begin to inhabit a garden, possibilities open up that go far beyond the limitations of adult imagination. The mutable, improvised, and mysterious vestiges of a child's vision of the garden—odd piles of sticks, bridges, campsites—while they might make the garden sometimes untidy, also imbue it with magic.

I have noticed that children do not really want or need large pieces of fixed prefabricated play equipment. The key to their garden happiness is the opportunity to invent their own worlds. For the youngest ones, bliss is a box of sand in which to make pies or just part of a bed where they are allowed to burrow like moles. As they grow a little older, a corner of the woodpile with some sawed-up sections of tree trunk and a few boards will quickly become a fort, then a ship, then a castle, then another planet altogether. Any tree that can be climbed, will be, and a long swing from a high branch or perhaps a rope ladder will cement the child-tree relationship forever. Any part of the garden that is left even a little wild and unexpected, the shrubs unpruned, grass unmown, or if occasionally a rabbit or a deer runs through it, or an owl or coyote can be heard at night, that section will be particularly compelling to a child, even if, or especially if, he or she is also a bit afraid of it.

Usually children spend more time in the garden than anybody else. It is where they learn about the world, because they can be in it unsupervised, yet protected. Some gardeners will remember from their own earliest recollections that no one sees the garden as vividly, or cares about it as passionately, as the child who grows up in it. That intensity haunts the garden long after the parent has picked up the final Matchbox toy on a summer evening, or discovered the last twig-and-acorn elf house, and long after that child has grown up and become the gardener.

Chapter 2 Preparing the Ground

To-day I think
Only with scents,—scents dead leaves yield,
And bracken, and wild carrot's seed,
And the square mustard field;

Odours that rise
When the spade wounds the root of tree,
Rose, currant, raspberry, or goutweed,
Rhubarb or celery;

The smoke's smell too,
Flowing from where a bonfire burns
The dead, the waste, the dangerous,
And all to sweetness turns.

It is enough
To smell, to crumble the dark earth,
While the robin sings over again
Sad songs of Autumn mirth.

Edward Thomas, "Digging"

When one is first beginning to garden, or gardening in a place one does not yet know, soil can seem dumb and unhelpful, just dirt. It is gray and empty, or yellow, clammy, and stony, or perhaps it is black and full of worms. Little pebbles might be interspersed all through it, or big ones, or maybe there is a rock ledge a spade's depth away. The plants thrive or languish in mysterious ways.

As one begins to work in it, a sense of the soil sharpens. One gets to know its grit or muddiness, its smell and warmth or chill, how it holds or drains water, what creatures inhabit it. One might notice how these qualities connect with each other, how they

show themselves in the ways the plants grow. Most of all one discovers that the soil does not stay the same, but, like anything alive, is always changing and telling its own story.

Soil is the substance of transformation. It brings about change while it is itself continually changing. This is why when one meets a new garden it is at first difficult to hear what it says. It is important to pause and watch for a while, to find out what is really going on, what needs to be done.

Soil work is done when not much is growing, in autumn or early spring. Leaves have fallen off the trees, bare stalks stick out of the borders. Few birds sing and the ground smells of rot. The work can be heavy and when it gets too dark to see, it is time to go inside to scrub off the mud. Muscles ache, but there is the glow of places that are stiff and lifeless yielding, opening to possibility, coming into being.

Aeons ago wind, rain, and sun gnarled the surface of smooth new rock. Lichens and mosses pioneered the crevices. Dead lichen reacted with mineral matter, giving rootholds to other plants, which, growing and rotting in turn, invited more tiny organisms. Animals foraged through, leaving their droppings and remains. All this interactivity—subterranean and celestial, organic and inorganic—went on throughout the millennia creating the subsoils, topsoils, and humus of today, the soils that have died and blown away as dust and the soils that are still being made. To cultivate the soil in one's own small plot is to continue that process, participating in a kind of alchemy wherein what once was dead is brought to life.

Kinds of soil

It is common and useful to classify soil according to whether it is sand, clay, or loam. By taking note of the look, feel, and smell of the stuff, and of how it behaves as one begins to work it, one discovers which it is and what it needs.

A sandy soil is made up of relatively large particles, big enough that in a pinch of soil one can feel each grain; they sometimes glint in the sun. Clay is made of many tiny particles, too small to see or feel. Squeeze it in your fingers and it will stick, cool and clammy and dark. Loam is often moist and will crumble into interesting grainy lumps.

If the soil you are digging is sandy, the spade will slide in easily. Silica, which predominates in sandy soil, reflects light and holds heat. In spring, seeds germinate quickly and plants grow fast because the soil is quick to warm up. Water runs through easily, often too easily, draining away into the subsoil and beyond the reach of plant roots. A sandy garden needs to be watered often. Water also carries nutrients, and these too leach away to where they cannot be used. Plants in a sandy garden tend to be thin and scraggly, quick to flower and go to seed. A sandy garden can be arid, desertlike.

If a sandy garden is light and warm and quick, a clay one is dense, heavy, and cold. Digging a clay garden is hard work, lugging spadefuls of clammy lumps. After rain, it can be days before the soil dries out enough to be worked without risking compaction. (In a sandy garden one seldom need wait more than a few hours.) Puddles linger. In hot weather the surface of a clay soil bakes into an impenetrable hard crust. Clay holds both water and nutrients, but can be so dense that the plants have trouble getting through to reach what they need. Without pockets and tunnels of air in the soil, plant roots are stifled and stunted. It takes a long time for anything to happen in a clay garden; plants grow slowly and laboriously.

Loam combines the qualities of sand and clay. Moist but not clammy, it crumbles easily into fragile lumps. It smells like a rainy morning in the woods, pungent and alive. There may be fragments of partially decomposed plants, and probably earthworms. Loam holds water well, without compacting or forming puddles. Between its crumbs there is air and room for plant roots to travel freely and find what they need. In a loamy garden, plants unfold steadily, realizing the full potentiality of each stage of their growth. Sometimes one is given a loamy garden, but usually the gardener must create it.

Clay and sand are the two extremes and loam the golden

mean, so one might assume that the remedy for one would be to balance it with some of the other. One might sometimes add a little sand to a clay soil and vice versa, but the benefit is usually short-lived. Mechanistic remedies seldom work in gardens, unless one is building a wall. The way genuinely to change the nature of a soil is to handle it gently, the way one would a plant or animal, and to add humus. This allows the soil to change itself.

Humus, the life of the soil

Humus is organic matter that is rotting, in transition between kingdoms. Imagine a redwood forest. Trees tower three hundred feet above the ground, their needlelike leaves soaking in light from the sun and turning it into still more greenness. On the forest floor below is a thick layer of fallen needles, decaying ferns, mushrooms, birds' egg shells, the corpses of squirrels and voles, here and there a rotting branch or trunk invaded by ants. This litter is what has sustained those mighty trees for two, three, perhaps four thousand years. It is humus.

In a garden, especially a garden of annual plants that are pulled out every year, very little is left to rot on the ground, and so the soil becomes more and more lifeless, more mineral, less animal or vegetable. It will become more sandy, if that is its tendency, or more clayey, if it is that way inclined. If humus is not replaced, the soil will become inanimate: nothing will grow except the stubbornest weeds.

Finding ways to restore humus to the soil, to continue the cycle of life rather than to deplete it in dust, has always been the essential—though hidden—art of gardening. There are many different ways to do it and gardeners find their own, according to the particular needs of their own gardens and lives. Traditionally they have used the manure of grass-eating animals: humus that is already well digested, concentrated, and readily absorbed. Manure is not so easy to come by these days; gardens need it but can seldom get enough. Mulches and cover crops (plantings of particular legumes or grasses to protect and enrich the soil; see chapter 6) also bring life to the soil. Compost is another form of intensified humus-making, and recipes for various composts can be found in the next chapter. Gardeners in some situations—with tiny gardens or in cities—may have to be quite ingenious in finding ways to make and use them. But it can be done, and there can be fascination in the doing.

Most methods of adding humus require spending time with amorphous substances like sod and weeds, tea leaves, and wet straw. Once in a while gardeners may have to get damp and overheated, possibly smelly. They need to notice small changes, be generally alert and able to improvise. In exchange for this muddy work one gets a living soil and a direct initiation into the way things are.

Humus works in two ways. First it creates good tilth—the soil structure through which plants receive water and nutrients. Humus also enables plants to absorb the full *range* of nutrients they need to grow, the mineral ones as well as the organic. Plants have no stomachs; they need humus instead.

When humus is added to a clay soil, it becomes lighter; spaces open through which plant roots can travel freely. To a sandy soil, humus brings substance and weight, the ability to hold water and nutrients. That these things happen is not simply the result of adding physical bulk—leaf mold or compost. The real transformation in texture and consistency happens more slowly, caused by the activity of tiny organisms. These living beings bind together mineral particles with organic matter to form aggregates, the lumps and crumbs and colloids that form a perfect soil. A good soil's sweet scent is the odor of work in progress.

An agricultural adage says the tiny animals that live below the surface of a healthy pasture weigh more than the cows grazing above it. In a catalogue selling composting equipment I read that two handfuls of healthy soil contain more living organisms than there are people on the earth. What these beings are and what they can be doing is difficult to even begin to comprehend, but it helps to realize that even though they are many, they work as one.

Some of these creatures one can see with the naked eye; others can be recognized by their effects. Starting with those one can see, there are worms, beetles, centipedes, grubs, mites. Next in order of decreasing size but not significance come the fungi and algae. The green strands one sometimes sees on the soil's surface are the algae; fungi are the delicate white filaments within the soil (they also manifest above the ground as mushrooms and toadstools after a rain). Flagellates and ciliates are single-celled animals, too small to see. Then, in untold numbers and variety, continually in flux and change, come actinomycetes and other bacteria, minute organisms existing somewhere between plant and animal.

All these organisms flock to the corpses of flora and fauna and transform them into carbon and nitrogen and all the other substances, many still unknown, that create new plant growth. They do not do this as individual entities, but collectively as a sensitive, transformative web. The fungi, algae, and insects begin the process of breaking down dead leaves, petals, mouse bodies. The worms continue, carrying substances below the surface of the soil and creating rich, new compounds in their own castings. Bacteria sort and refine in the subtlest ways, acting as the digestive system of the plants, and as antibiotics, warding off disease and imbalance. Some fungi and bacteria live in symbiosis with plant roots, penetrating into their very cells to transmit substances the plants could not otherwise absorb.

When a soil is alive like this, it "knows" what the plants need and can provide it. It is receptive, changing and adapting to the subtlest movements of weather, seasons, and stars. Fertile soil is called "in good heart."

Chemical fertilizers?

Biologists have only recently established that a living soil is not so much a random collection of worms and microbes as a powerful phenomenon of intelligent interrelatedness. But such a view is nothing new. The legends of Demeter and Persephone, Isis and Osiris, remind us that throughout history the earth was understood to be alive and wise, a being to be feared and respected. It was only recently, beginning a hundred and fifty years ago, that chemists developed the ability to analyze the substances that seemed to nourish plants, synthesize them in test tubes, and pour them back into the soil to yield bigger crops with less labor. This was the beginning of a different picture: the soil as null, an empty medium through which to deliver scientifically reduced substances to plants.

Since this is a book about gardening, not agriculture, it is not the place to debate chemical versus organic farming. But I do want to point out why contemplative gardeners might find chemical fertilizers fundamentally uninteresting.

Artificial fertilizers did, in some ways, fulfill their promise; they let crops grow where otherwise they would not, and they saved the labor of restoring organic matter to the soil. But when they were used with less than the utmost restraint, chemicals applied to the soil upset the intricate relationships among soil creatures—an effect that was neither foreseen nor at first understood to be a problem. To quiet farmers' concerns that worms were leaving their fields, the USDA pronounced in 1957, "Earthworms are the sign of a healthy soil, not a cause." Nonetheless, the worms withered or fled. Useful bacteria and fungi, finding themselves redundant, disappeared and made room for forms that were less benign. A description of the soil as a lifeless medium resulted in soils that became that way. Fields lost tilth and adaptability (and the local character that made a bean grown in one region taste different from the same kind of bean grown in another), became dependent on chemicals for fertility and resistance, were no longer in good heart.

One can grow a pretty enough garden with chemical fertilizers, but I would not want to. Without soil life, plants cannot take in the full range of subtle nutrients, nor the influence of sky and stars: lettuce will be without delicacy of flavor, carrots will lack robustness. The red rose may unfold its velvet petals, but not its deepest tones of rose scent. Fewer butterflies and bees will flit through the garden air. Fewer birds will come for fewer worms. Since it is all a matter of degree, it is possible one might not notice. What will be gone is the chance to witness and abet—slowly, and sometimes only after many mistakes—renewal and transformation at work.

Soil chemistry and organic amendments

Because working organically in the garden (primarily adding humus) means that one is taking care of both the soil structure and its chemical constituents at the same time, gardeners who prefer not to think in terms of phosphorus, nitrogen, and potassium can often avoid them. I was such a gardener for most of my gardening life. The garden I moved into seventeen years ago had not really been gardened for several decades. But it had been "landscaped" by a service that mowed the lawn and year after year took away all the grass clippings and raked the leaves and hauled them off to the dump. What remained was a long, parched, yellow lawn under high-branched but melancholy oaks, with a few elongated shrubs along the edges: the whole place exuded the lifelessness and anonymity of an exhausted city park. It was so sad I could hardly bear to see it. My test holes revealed a soil like gray cement, wormless, even grubless.

All my soil-feeding efforts for the first years went into recycling every ounce of organic matter I could find—leaves, weeds, scraps, manure—almost anything that had once been alive. (The way I did this is described in the next chapter, on composting, but probably more rough-and-ready methods would also have worked.) That first autumn I also planted daffodil bulbs and crocus corms (bulbs come with their own nutrients and will grow almost anywhere), which, when they bloomed, cheered not only me but also the garden, bringing bees and early butterflies. The effect of a little humus on my starved soil was dramatic: every year more kinds of plants thrived, insects hummed, rabbits scampered, and birds sang where once there had been a dreadful stillness. And naturally the more plants grew, both planned and unplanned, the more substance there was to give back to the soil. For ten years I never thought to test the soil's nutrient content—the nitrogen, phosphorus, potassium—with a soil test; though I may once have measured its pH. The garden was coming to life and that was enough.

There are gardeners who either develop, or possess from the beginning, a quick understanding of what a surfeit or deficiency of one or the other of soil's chemical constituents means for the plants in the garden. They know in their fingertips that, for instance, phosphorus is related to the flowering process in plants, potassium to rooting. Their gardening is enhanced—just as mine is often confused—by a specific knowledge of the chemical constituents of their soil.

Some garden books recommend as a first step in caring for the soil that gardeners send away for soil tests that tell in precise numbers what the acidity or alkalinity of the soil is, and how much of which plant nutrients are present at the time of the test. On the whole, I believe that such analyses can be useful as long as they are used together with—never instead of—one's own perceptions of the garden as it grows and changes. Some gardeners might enjoy using soil tests year by year as a comparison with, or deepening of, their own observations. But others may be made so anxious by the little printed-out numbers and abbreviations that they can no longer trust what they see and smell. Any gardeners who notice this happening to them should throw away their tests at once. No good, and certainly no delightful, gardening can be done when gardeners no longer trust their own senses.

Some gardeners feel more confident beginning work in a new garden with a soil test in hand. Others prefer to feel their way in for a few years and may never test their soil. Soil tests are never necessary unless problems develop to which there is no obvious solution. Then tests may help, but only if one realizes what they are and what they are not.

Most simple soil tests measure the quantities of plant nutrients present at the moment of that test and the pH of the soil: its relative acidity or alkalinity. Every plant needs its nitrogen, potassium, and phosphorus, not to mention its magnesium, calcium, and sulfur, and minute traces of iron, copper, and zinc, to name just a few known necessities. And every soil must somehow supply them. But the way these elements behave in life is not like a jigsaw puzzle to which a gardener can simply supply the missing pieces. Rather they engage in a continually changing dance—a dance to which the nature of the plants grown, the way the soil is handled, the hours of sunlight, and the fluctuations of rain, wind, and stars provide the music.

There are reasons why most of the time more compost and manure, with occasional rests and green manures, are the best solutions when the plants in a garden seem undernourished despite healthy amounts of sunlight, water, and weeding. In good compost, plant nutrients are already dancing, joined by microorganisms into dynamic forms that the roots of plants can absorb.

If, after the soil has been enriched for several seasons with compost or manure, certain plants still do not want to grow, or all the plants seem less than radiant, persevering gardeners might be able to pinpoint the nature of the deficiency either by sending for a soil test, or by carefully observing the plants and consulting a book that describes the symptoms of various deprivations. In such a book they will learn, for instance, that poor leaf growth may be a mark of too little nitrogen, or that plants that flourish but are slow to come to flower may be suffering from phosphorus deficiency. (*Start with the Soil* by Grace Gershuny is very useful guide, clear without oversimplification.) They can then investigate appropriate organic soil amendments to address the situation: perhaps kelp meal for potassium, more manure or fish emulsion for nitrogen, bone meal for phosphorus.

Such soil amendments are called organic because the mineral elements they contain already form part of living compounds and are therefore more balanced and absorbable than synthetic chemical products. Some garden centers supply these products, and suggestions for reliable mail-order catalogues, with clear descriptions of contents and uses, may be found in the Readings and Resources section at the end of this book. Although gardeners are fortunate in being able to obtain such valuable substances, they still need to use them with caution. In as complex and delicate a matter as a living soil, a little knowledge can be a dangerous thing.

It is not enough to have plenty of the right nutrients in a soil; each nutrient must be in the proper proportion to the others or the plants cannot absorb it. If, for example, a soil has too much magnesium in it (perhaps as a result of too much added wood ash) the calcium will be locked up: it will be for the plants as though the calcium were not there. It is therefore best to work slowly with amendments, using conservative quantities, and it is safer to add them to a compost heap than to scatter them directly on the soil. The compost organisms have a balancing effect and render the mineral substances into forms plant roots can digest (this is what is called chelation). Some hints about what one might add to the compost, and when, are given in chapter 3.

The same approach—beginning with humus and adding other amendments only if really necessary—can be taken in the matter of adjusting a soil's pH. (Simple kits just for measuring soil pH can be found in hardware stores and many seed catalogues.) The pH factor is significant in a garden because if a soil is either extremely acid or extremely alkaline, then no matter what nutrients it contains, the plants will be unable to absorb them. The soil becomes sullen and is no longer lively. So the first step in correcting the situation is to wake the soil up. When one adds humus, the soil will become more active, whether it is acid or alkaline. Often this is all that is necessary to enable the plants to absorb what they need.

If after testing and adding compost, the soil is still too acid— the plants are not growing well and prevalent weeds are sorrel, knotweed, and bracken—you might carefully add a little lime in a gentle form such as oystershell or dolomitic limestone. (See chapter 6, on weeds as indicator plants.) If your soil tested as highly alkaline and after adding compost, the soil still is—the plants are not growing well and thistles and mustards are prevalent weeds— you might work a mulch of acidic plant materials, such as pine needles or oak leaves, into the top layer of the soil. If this still does not acidify the soil enough for the plants you want to grow, you can cautiously add gypsum (mined calcium sulfate). While it is possible to change the soil's pH in a single season to benefit a particular crop—to grow beets in the vegetable garden, or turn a hydrangea's blossoms from pink to blue—a significant long-term change in the soil itself will take a few years and happen most effectively with compost.

While it is reassuring to know that there are solutions for exigencies that can occur, most of the time contemplative gardeners need not be concerned with a detailed analysis of their soil, which in any case will never tell the whole story. Rather, they can move toward inclusiveness and synthesis: building up organic matter, letting in light, watering and weeding, cultivating carefully. Slowly but surely the garden will arrive at its own best balance.

Cultivation

Feeding a living soil is a matter of composts, mulches, and manures; but cultivating it depends on what one does with spade, fork, and hands. I used to wonder exactly when it was I was cultivating the soil. I was sure I was cultivating it when I dug over the beds, but did not yet know that sometimes I could be cultivating the soil by not digging it. To cultivate something—the soil or a friendship—means approaching it with attentiveness, with consideration of its nature. Almost every small garden job done in this way—weeding, watering, even strolling around and looking—becomes a cultivation and enlivening of the soil.

Gardens do need to be dug, at least in the beginning. Probably grass or brambles or weeds are growing where one wants to plant something else. Or perhaps there already is a garden bed, but the soil is tired and compacted and needs reawakening; loosening and aerating the soil always brings a quick surge of fertility. Roots from nearby trees or bushes might be invading and need to be dug out, or stones or bits of rubble. Sometimes one just needs to know what is down there.

These are all good reasons to dig, but there are also reasons to be cautious. The layer of soil that is pervaded by soil life is only at the top, no more than six inches deep, often only three or four. If in digging the garden one turns it upside down, burying the topsoil where it cannot be reached and bringing the inactive subsoil to the top, then one buries the garden's fertility. This is the reason for double digging, the traditional technique used by gardeners to bring air and moisture to both topsoil and subsoil without disturbing the soil's structure. In this method the top stays on the top, the bottom on the bottom, and at the end the garden bed rises from the ground as miraculously as kneaded bread from a bowl.

Double digging

Double digging ought to be called something else. It sounds onerous: digging but more so. One does need some strength, especially the first year, but no one should have to strain or feel bad. I am so puny that my children have to open jam jars for me, but I love digging the garden.

Much depends on timing and state of mind. The job can be done slowly, a little one day, a little the next, or perhaps even a little one year, a little the next. Digging the garden quickly, so one can get on to something else, can be exhausting. But contemplative gardeners do not usually hurry. Keeping in mind that digging is something one does only rarely—when making new beds for perennials and shrubs, possibly once a year in beds of annual flowers or vegetables—the occasion can take on a ceremonial quality that can be lingered over, even savored.

WHEN

The soil should not be opened during extremes of heat or cold. One digs close to the equinoxes, autumn or spring, when temperatures are moderate, days and nights of equal length, and the year is balanced, a bit hushed, holding its breath before tipping into the new season.

If one can manage to dig in autumn, the soil will have time to settle down over the winter and to receive the beneficial effects of frost. Frost is the best possible cultivator of a heavy clay soil. Each drop of water in such a soil will freeze and thaw all winter long, alternately expanding and contracting, causing the heavy clods to break down, till, by spring, it is loose and friable. Frost is the great cleanser, ridding the soil of toxic root secretions, unwanted insects, and plant diseases. If one has to wait till spring, then it is best to dig early enough to let the beds rest for a few weeks before planting them.

HOW

Double digging is a job that should only be attempted with good tools; without them, even if one got started, one would soon give up. But the tools one needs are few: a spade, a fork, and a wheelbarrow. The spade should be the kind that can be sharpened to a knifelike edge. It should have a handle that is comfortable to hold and is neither so short that one hunches over it nor so long as to be in the way. The fork must be strong enough not to break halfway through the job. It is helpful to setting up a good working rhythm if spade and fork are of a similar size and weight—like a knife and fork—since one is constantly shifting from one to the other. Any wheelbarrow will do.

I have divided the process into numbered steps for the sake of clarity, but readers should not be intimidated. It is really quite simple.

1. With the edge of the spade mark out the outline of your future bed. Bear in mind that you will not want to walk on it, so it should be a size that you can easily reach across. Four feet is the maximum, assuming you can reach in from both sides.

2. Scatter compost or rotted manure on the surface; this will be incorporated as you dig. (If you are digging up grass, add the compost at the end.)

3. Taking up the spade, dig a trench across the width of the bed, one spade's depth deep and a spadeful wide. Toss the soil you dig out into the wheelbarrow; you will need it later. If you are digging up grass, you will need to stop to shake the good topsoil out of the roots into the barrow, and to pile the grass to one side to put in the compost later. (This can be wearisome, but it only has to be done once.)

4. With your fork, loosen the soil at the bottom of the trench as deep as the fork will go. Work your way across the trench. This is when you are likely to meet rocks and roots or old bottles that need to be pulled out.

5. Dig a second trench next to the first one. Spade the topsoil from the second trench onto the loosened subsoil of the first.

6. Loosen the subsoil of the second trench with the fork.

7. Continue this process, working through to the end.

8. When you have loosened the subsoil of the last trench, take the wheelbarrow of topsoil saved from the first trench and spade it into the last one.

Now the bed is made. Bare earth rises up in clods waiting to be planted; worms wriggle through, small grubs tumble among the lumps. A few upturned roots, pebbles, and the skeletons of leaves may be made out here and there; but there is no color, hardly any form, no roses, no turnips, just possibility.

If you dig in the fall, the beds should not be left bare over winter. A light mulch lets the frost's crystallizing force penetrate the soil while preventing the topsoil from drying out and blowing away in the wind. The mulch could be compost, leaf mold, seaweed. Dead leaves would also work, but not pure oak leaves, which would make the soil too acid.

HOW OFTEN

It would be convenient if there were rules about how often to dig. Some schools of gardening are adamant about double digging every year, and others are equally convincing about "no till"—no digging, ever, but lots of mulch. Probably both systems could be made to work in certain circumstances if one tried hard enough. On the whole I believe it is best to decide for oneself, based on what one can see in one's own garden, keeping a balance between letting the soil get heavy and stagnant from lack of movement at one extreme and stirring it up so much that it gets dry and lifeless on the other. Gardeners get a sense for this over time, handling and watching, moving toward soil that is crumbly and worm-filled, and plants that thrive.

As a general guideline, if the soil is a very heavy clay, a vegetable garden or annual bed might benefit from being dug every year at the beginning of its life. This situation will not continue indefinitely. The more one heaps on compost, the lighter the soil will become. But in many cases, and certainly where the soil tends to be sandy, one must be careful not to dig too often. As long as one is adding compost to the garden, it is better to break up the soil as little as possible, allowing the organic connections among aggregates and colloids to thrive undisturbed. Letting aeration take place that way, instead of with a spade and fork, one might easily go five or six years between diggings, especially if one is attentive to rotations and rests, unless invading tree roots are a problem.

Tree roots seek out rich soil and water and invade cultivated beds. They rob the plants of nourishment and stunt them with uncongenial secretions, so they must be dug out. Sometimes, just digging over a small section is enough to get at an offending root, but all too often, one ends up turning over the whole bed.

A way to compensate for too much digging, and also indeed for too much cropping (as in my tired vegetable bed), is to dig early enough in the fall to plant a cover crop of clover or a legume, a "green manure." (Cover crop seeds are available from good vegetable seed catalogues.) The bacteria that surround the roots of these plants will do much to restore the soil's internal connections. How long to leave the cover crop growing depends on how long you can spare the growing space and on the life cycle of the cover plant. Perhaps it will be just till spring. Then you dig the bed over, and incorporate the plants, root and leaf and all, in the soil. (You must wait a couple of weeks before planting, allowing the soil to digest.)

In those autumns when the garden does not need digging, one

simply pulls out any weeds, then mulches well with compost or manure, which the worms will dig in. In spring all that will be needed is a gentle raking to prepare the seedbed, and the garden year is ready to begin again.

A NOTE ON PERENNIAL BEDS

In perennial beds and shrub borders, the plants will put down roots to stay. One prepares such beds in the same way as for annual plantings—the vegetables and tender flowers—only more thoroughly and deeply, since this will be the only chance. The organic matter should be dug in deeply, to six or eight inches. This is the time to search for cow manure and to use one's very best compost; a handful or two of bone meal per square yard is also good for flowers.

When formal gardens were staffed by teams of scurrying gardeners, perennial beds used to be dug up and remade every three or four years, the plants replanted or divided, the soil fertilized. Such a task is beyond most part-time gardeners. Instead the bed will be renewed bit by bit as one moves plants around and divides or adds new ones, shoveling some compost and bone meal into the holes as one goes, scattering more as a mulch in between. Many plants are happy to be left in peace, casting their leaves, petals, and seeds onto an undisturbed soil.

A biodynamic refinement: soil spray

At the moment in spring when most of my vegetable beds are prepared (dug, if they are going to be, then covered with compost and raked) but not yet planted, and when only the first few green and pink shoots of perennials show through the earth, I like to lightly cover the soil with something called horn manure spray. This is a kind of soil medicine developed in Switzerland and Germany in the 1920s by the Austrian philosopher Rudolf Steiner for a circle of farmers concerned about diminished soil fertility and poor germination of seeds that seemed to be resulting from an increasingly mechanized approach to farming. This group began what became a worldwide movement called biodynamics. Biodynamics, though its public image is sometimes mystified as a bit occult and arcane, is essentially about applying, in practical ways, observations of the subtle and lively forces of nature to the farm and garden in order to reenliven soil and plants.

I came across biodynamics very early in my gardening life, by stumbling onto the literature and by marrying a farmer who used its methods. I was surprised to discover that its at first obscure and difficult-to-understand observations actually sharpened and confirmed my intuitive delight in nature and in watching a garden grow, once I began to grasp them. They called on me to make conscious what I had thought of as vague atmosphere, glimpses out of the corner of my eye—the gesture of an unfolding leaf, how and where a hoar frost settles on the ground—and begin to "read" these elusive phenomena, even to make use of them. My husband and I studied the books in print and went to lectures. He took what he learned out to the farm. I went to our small garden, where I applied the methods where I could as I watched my flowers grow and learned to grow vegetables for the children. I still persist, sometimes following the letter of instruction, mostly attempting what is for me biodynamics' most profound injunction—to truly see what one sees.

In any event, the particular spray that Rudolf Steiner recommended be put on the soil before planting is called horn manure because it is prepared by taking fresh cow manure and tightly packing it into the horn of a cow, as a container in which it is buried underground for a whole winter. The manure becomes composted manure, but an intensified version.

All compost is made in part by being given a kind of form (usually it is piled into a heap) and by paying attention to weather and the time of year. The significance of form—not in opposition to, but in interaction with the analysis of substance—is central to biodynamic thought as a way to understand the nature of living things. This compost is given a very particular form by its package: the horn of the soulful, ruminative cow. Steiner offered a picture of a cow horn as that which contains and concentrates what it holds within, as opposed to a stag's antler, which, antennalike, might be seen as an organ of perception reaching outward. The filled horn is buried in winter, because winter is the time when nature's activity is strongest beneath the surface of the earth. This specialized compost is dug out in the spring, mixed with water, and sprayed on the ground. Its particular purpose is to transform the most lifeless, most mineral aspect of the soil in order to create a more vital environment for seeds to germinate and for roots to take hold. This is why one sprays it before most of the spring planting is done.

Farmers who have cows often make this manure spray themselves, but gardeners can order it from the Josephine Porter Institute in Woolwine, Virginia, a not-for-profit organization named to honor a small, iron-willed woman who, for thirty years, made this preparation and seven others on a small farm in Pennsylvania, supplying them by mail at tiny cost to whoever wanted them (see chapters 3 and 10 on using these preparations, and Reading and Resources for ordering information). I once met her and still remember her sweet smile. Now this work is being done at Woolwine, so gardeners may still send for supplies. When the horn manure preparation comes through the mail in its little plastic bag, it is a dark, crumbly substance with no smell. The amount sent to cover a whole acre is not even a quarter of a cup. This spray works homeopathically, tiny doses having powerful effects.

To apply it to the soil, the horn manure must first be well distributed through approximately three gallons of water. This is done by stirring it for an hour—with one's hand as the stirrer—in a bucket or barrel. The technique is to stir in one direction till the mixture in the bucket spirals into a vortex (once again the form tells the story) then to stir the other way till the vortex reappears, continuing back and forth. When the hour is over, it is sprayed at once onto bare soil, using a sprayer or simply a little whisk broom of twigs or stiff straw with which one flicks out thousands of little drops. It is a quiet, meditative business, staring into the barrel for an hour, then carefully circumambulating the garden with the brush, making sure all bare earth is covered. It is done as well as, not instead of, all the regular spreading of composting and manure. Each year I think I will not have time for it, but then somehow I do.

Watering and weeding

It is a garden paradox that soil without good tilth cannot hold moisture, while soil that lacks moisture cannot be in good tilth. Just watering is not enough, and too much water can be harmful as well as wasteful. Good cultivation can help the soil make the best use of what water there is.

Liberty Bailey once wrote that "we may water the garden with a rake." If the soil's surface is compacted and hard, water cannot penetrate; it will stay on top and evaporate before it reaches the plants. Bailey recommends, as most gardeners of his generation did, that one keep stirring the top of the soil to create a rough surface that will be receptive to air and moisture. It does not matter if the surface of the soil feels a bit dry to the touch; the moisture is needed a few inches below. Always dig a little hole and feel before deciding it is time to water. A good tool for soil-stirring is one with three small, fingerlike prongs on a long handle, called a cultivator.

People who worry about disturbing the humus layer hesitate to be always scratching at the top of the soil. I myself find that a little soil-stirring in spring, when seeds are just sprouting, enlivens the garden. Later on, as the sun gets hotter, soil gets stirred enough when I pull out weeds. As summer comes, little bare earth is exposed to the sky because most of the soil is shaded by leaves— the leaves of my plants and those of the weeds I did not get around to pulling out. This green shade is the best protection against baking and evaporation. In the time between harvesting a late spring crop and a new fall one growing up, the soil will be suddenly bare again in the baking heat. Then I cover it with the lightest mulch, grass clippings and faded flowers. This too is cultivation.

Plow soles and footprints

I have never used a gas-powered tiller. Perhaps I would have if the garden had been very difficult to turn over at the very beginning, or if it had been important to have a lot of new garden beds all at once. But this was not the case, so I was happy to dig bit by bit.

If one can manage it, working by hand is better for both the soil and the gardener. A tilling machine cannot substitute for double digging because it does not go as deep. At the same time, the machine is more powerful than a spade and can pulverize the top layer of the soil. Further, using a mechanical tiller year after year tends to compact the ground beneath the surface, creating a hard, impenetrable layer called a plow sole.

Not every gardener shares my lack of ease with machines in the garden. I think it would take me longer to rent a rototiller and figure out how to work it than to dig almost anything. But even the technically adept could not enjoy the noise or the gas smell. Digging is almost silent; the quiet crunch of the spade mingles with the chirps of crickets and the songs of birds. Birds and tranquillity vanish with a motor's roar.

There are certain situations in which tilling is helpful: for instance, moving into an abandoned garden where deep-rooted brambles and weeds really make digging too difficult. To gain a foothold I would rent a rototiller, perhaps with a person to run it, for the first cultivation. This would have to be repeated once or twice more as the roots reasserted themselves, until the plants gave up. Then I would apologize for all the violence and make amends by planting a deep-rooted green manure crop.

Speaking of footholds, I realize that I have forbidden walking on garden beds, but have not fully explained why. A carefully placed bare footprint between plants now and then will not hurt, but if garden soil is repeatedly walked on it will become compacted and lifeless. This is why one tries to keep garden beds to sizes and shapes one can reach into.

My vegetable beds are all of a size I can comfortably sit beside to sow seeds, or weed, or thin. I enjoy this very much, sometimes lapsing into reveries or even naps, the scent of warm soil and chamomile entering my dreams. The flower beds are more of a problem, because I cannot seem to restrain myself from making them wider every year to make room for more flowers I want to get to know. I could not possibly reach into them anymore, so I have to walk in to weed or pick things. I find that with a few flat rocks as stepping stones, at least I always walk on the same places. Certain small plants like to cool their roots under these rocks, and children use them too, because they love jumping from one to the other and hiding inside the garden.

Chapter 3 Compost

Making compost is rather like living. If you wait until you can do a perfect job, you'll never get started. Better to make a start and learn as you go.

Ann Mendenhall

If you are a good organic gardener, looking at a rose you can see the garbage, looking at the garbage you can see a rose.

Thich Nhat Hanh, *Peace Is Every Step*

This chapter is about making compost, an activity I happen to very much enjoy. But it must be said at the outset that there are many ways to make a garden, and I would not want to depress any new gardeners, or unsettle any old ones, with the thought that if they do not make compost their gardens will fail. It will always be true that "the footsteps of the gardener make the best fertilizer." Loving attention makes a garden sing. There are leaf molds and organic soil amendments, and in some communities entrepreneurs sell composted horse or cow manure, gold for the garden. Some gardeners will take these routes to a healthy garden and they can skip this chapter, or come back to it later. But I would wish that every gardener would at least briefly entertain the notion that compost-making might have an attraction all its own.

There is an allure, both practical and philosophical, in the notion that not only is there a single substance that can give the garden all the fertility it needs, but also that the gardener participates in its making. In his lively and wise *Second Nature,* Michael Pollan argues that American gardeners' fascination with compost has to do with morality. He says they like making compost because it makes them feel they are being good, whereas British gardeners are heartless aesthetes who don't care. As a gardener who began in England and went on in America, I see what Pollan means, but I believe that in this case he has missed the point. I would urge all contemplative gardeners to try a compost heap sometime—not in spite of the work, but actually because of it.

Compost-making is another garden job; it is not picking roses, but in its earthy way it can engage the soul as much. It isn't simple; hardly anyone gets it right at first. One fiddles and struggles,

mixing the molds and peels, carting manure, mixing what is fresh and green with what is aged and yellow, paying attention to wet and dry, hot and cold, sour and sweet. But in this job, more perhaps than in any other, the sense emerges of what it is beneath one's feet and in the air that makes the garden grow. Weaving endings with beginnings, gardeners glimpse what they cannot see.

The heaps

It can be confusing to hear gardeners discussing *the* compost heap, as though there were only one. There actually needs to be two. One heap is the stockpile into which all the debris of the garden and kitchen goes higgledy-piggledy in no order except what comes to hand. Whatever is clipped, weeded, raked, peeled— gone-to-seed lettuces, carrot tops, flower-bed edgings, seaweed washed up by a storm—along with all the contents of the kitchen bucket, tea leaves, onion skins, fish heads:* all are piled in a heap, with the help, perhaps, of a fork kept nearby to keep things in bounds. The only exception is brush—woody branches and twigs, tough stalks of cabbages or sunflowers. And if there are very many autumn leaves, some might be better left out. (In my garden, where there are fifteen large trees, I heap most of my leaves

---

*Some people leave their meat scraps out of the compost altogether, as they can attract rats and raccoons, and in a small garden, especially in a city, this might be necessary. But when there are occasional gristly bones in my kitchen bucket, I simply bury them deep in the pile with the fork. In summer I cover the scraps with leaves and earthy weeds, in winter with leaf mold and soil from a heap I keep for that purpose. It is a small extra effort, but a trace of animal remains is good for the compost. Moreover, household garbage is much easier and more pleasant to deal with when bones go to the garden.

into a separate leaf pile, where they turn into leaf mold, a good mulch and seed starter.)

The other pile is a much tidier, potent-looking mound, smaller, more compact, and covered with a thin coat of straw or leaves. This pile is in the process of becoming compost. To make it, once or twice a year gardeners take the contents of their stock-pile, hose them down, and layer them in a particular order, adding a few special ingredients in between. This assembly might take a morning to do. In a day or two the new heap will palpably heat up for a few days or a week, then cool down. Under the straw skin intricate work continues for several months, but it is no longer the gardeners who are doing it.

When the compost is ready to use, usually four to six months after the pile is assembled, it is dark and moist, a little lumpy, but with its component parts—leaves, stems, peels—no longer recognizable. Each shovelful reveals a worm or two still at work. Gardeners spread most of it over the surface of all their beds, while it is still rich and lively. I always try not to use it all at once, but hold some back for exigencies: half a barrowful for a planting of late lettuce, a couple of shovelfuls to work in around the roots of a peony making a slow return after a hard winter.

Siting and timing

Compost heaps need light shade and good drainage so they will neither dry out nor become sodden from sitting in water. Beyond this, they should be placed where they are most convenient and where they will not offend the eye, but might even please it. The stockpile and the made pile can be kept together or apart.

Because I have a big garden, my stockpile gets big and unruly from time to time (although it is surprising how quickly it shrinks down again). Therefore I keep it as far as possible from the house, behind some bushes where it is almost out of sight. I have to walk two hundred yards with the wheelbarrow or kitchen bucket; it is a long way, and I tend to put it off, but then I usually find that I enjoy leaving a steamy kitchen or a too-heated conversation to empty the compost bucket under the stars.

I keep my assembled heap closer to the house because it must be within reach of a hose (for me this means wheelbarrowing my stockpile two hundred yards back up again when it's time to make the pile, but this does not take very long). My "made" pile is between a hazel bush and an elder,* and is more in the public view, but I find it quite attractive with its leafy skin; it is a little hillock or tumulus, almost a landscape feature.

Gardeners with small gardens do not have room for big straggly piles, but neither do they need them. For one thing, small gardens produce less debris, so there is not so much to pile up. For another, with a pretty frame to hold things together, it is possible to keep everything tidy and aesthetic. Old cabbages no longer roll

---

*Both folk tradition and modern biochemistry recommend that elder, hazel, or birch, the roots of which encourage humus manufacture and good drainage, be planted near the compost pile. Planting hazels, birches, and elders is a refinement, not a necessity. Still, my hazel bush has grown to twenty feet and casts a lovely dappled shade, and the compost has been dark, sweet, and rich. One can get tiny hazels or little elders by mail for around ten dollars. Hazels have catkins that dance in light breezes, and, if one plants two varieties, there will be nuts, although usually the squirrels get them first. Elders, on the other hand, are said to come with a kind of dryad called the Hylde-Moer, or Elder Mother, who lives in the tree and wards off malevolence. Elders also grow lovely white flowers, which can be made into fritters to eat at midsummer.

away; there is a pleasant sense of rustic order. While composting containers are unnecessary in a large garden, they can be helpful in a small one. They consolidate and condense; furthermore, in compacting the material, a container can help a pile heat up, something that can be a problem if materials are scant.

There could be two containers, one for the stockpile and one for the assembled pile; or one might just use a container for the stockpile and make the assembled pile out in the open. If one is going to make compost in a container, one side should be removable or hinged so that the gardener can easily turn the pile while it is making and get at the compost once it is ready. There should be no floor, as the compost must be in contact with the earth, and the sides should let air in so the pile can breathe. The simplest design is probably a light wood-frame pen with chicken-wire walls divided into two sections. But the design and materials should really be whatever fits best into the particular garden. It is quite unnecessary for a compost container to be ugly. Gardeners who want to buy something ready-made can find several simple mail-order models made of cedar slats (see Readings and Resources section), which cost no more than the black plastic ones but are much more in keeping with a garden, and will become even more so with age.

To know when it is time to stop piling up weeds and leaves and start making compost, one needs to consider how much has been collected, the season, and the weather. It is one of the mysterious facts of composting that heaps below a certain size will not heat up. The minimum size for a finished pile is roughly four feet wide by four feet long by three feet high. One can manage with slightly less if one is making compost in a container. It seems that the compost creatures require that much mass to make the concerted effort that causes radical transformation.

In gardens with big trees or a serious vegetable patch, there is often enough plant debris to make compost twice a year. In small gardens, one needs to be resourceful and let nothing go to waste if one is going to gather enough material for one heap. If every stray leaf and blade is saved—beginning with the first spring cleaning—then even the tiniest garden can yield enough substance to make compost by the end of summer.

Late summer and early autumn are usually the best times for compost-making. Composting goes fast in warm weather, stops short when temperatures stay below freezing. But because compost-in-process must always stay a little moist, summers in many places are too dry. Early autumn is moist and fruitful, the stockpile loaded with faded annuals, overripe tomatoes, cut-back perennials, and summer weeds. As long as one can manage to build the pile with a month or two to spare before heavy frost sets in (if this happens in October, one can begin in August), autumn is an ideal time for compost-making, and the compost will be ready in time for spring planting.

Balancing the heap

Good compost needs to be balanced in particular ways. It can happen that the garden and kitchen supply everything that is needed. More often, gardeners need to look for other substances as counterweights. Some of these can be collected and saved as they turn up; others must be hunted for around the time the pile is to be made.

The most critical balance in compost-making is between carbon and nitrogen, those constituents of everything that lives. A good finished compost, ready to wake up the soil, is said by soil chemists to have a ratio of about twelve parts of carbon to one of nitrogen. To achieve this ratio at the end of the composting process one needs to begin with a higher ratio of carbon to nitrogen, about thirty to one, as a lot of carbon is lost in the composting process.

Contemplative gardeners do not need to work with tables in their hands giving the precise carbon–nitrogen ratio of their compost ingredients. Good compost can be made with no knowledge of the terms of chemistry, as long as one develops a sense of the *qualities* that are needed, and how they must be balanced. Substances that are high in carbon are twiggy, yellow, skeletal, and dry, more dead than alive: straw, stalks, sawdust, dead leaves. Substances that have a lot of nitrogen are still green and moist, often animal in origin: fresh grass clippings, damp hay, dead mice, manure, green leaves, kitchen scraps.

A compost pile that has too high a ratio of nitrogen to carbon will be wet and give off the smell of old urine. This is the sign of excess nitrogen evaporating into the air as ammonia, instead of becoming bound in the compost where one needs it. To avoid this, one can add more old leaves, perhaps some sawdust, or go and buy a bale of straw. A pile with too much carbon, on the other hand, will take a long time to break down, and by the time it does, much of its goodness will have been lost. In most gardens the excess will run toward too much carbon. By far the best balancer of this situation is the manure of grazing animals.

MANURE AND HOW TO GET IT

Green plants that have gone through the digestive system of a cow—encountering heat, intestinal flora, and perhaps the gentle, ruminative soul of the cow herself—are in an almost ideal form to return and enliven the earth. A gardener who can get hold of a truckload of good cow manure every year could compost it and the garden would need little else. These days, fewer cows graze in fewer meadows and they are often farther and farther from the garden. The art of compost-making has evolved—and is still evolving, as domestic animals fade from everyday life—and allows one to manage with less. Twenty percent of cow manure in a compost pile will balance 80 percent of dry leafiness. Horse, chicken, and duck manure, though not quite as digested and refined as cow manure, are also highly concentrated forms of nitrogen that will enrich the pile. Master compost makers can make rich, balanced composts entirely out of plant materials. This is a new and delicate skill. One day perhaps all gardeners will be forced to learn to make compost without the help of animals. But I hope it will not be soon.

When we began making compost in our garden, we grazed a sweet heifer on the lawn. She kept the grass short and I wandered about daily with the wheelbarrow, carefully collecting her droppings. When the little calf raised her head to glimpse an egret flying over the pond, I was sure that what she saw would enter the compost, along with the sunlight that glinted on the water. In time, however, she was banned by a village ordinance disallowing cattle. Meanwhile, over a period of twenty years, the three dairy farms in our area were shut down by economic pressure to get big or get out. Fresh milk for children now travels two hundred miles.

But difficulty will not keep an avid compost maker from the quest. Within reasonable driving distance from my garden, a few individuals keep family cows; there are also two chicken farms with friendly farmers. I telephone first and ask permission to come over and scoop up a couple of garbage cans full. I always offer to pay: manure is valuable to farmers as well as to gardeners, though few will grudge a polite gardener a small amount. For manure gathering one needs a big bucket, a pitchfork, rubber boots, and the garbage cans. I find the hardest part to be the transfer of cow pats or chicken droppings from my bucket to the garbage cans, which are wedged into the back of my very small station wagon. This maneuver would be a lot easier with a truck; more difficult, but possible, with a two-door sedan.

Even though I always brace myself for such expeditions—the digging and hauling, the perhaps skittish cow—I have yet to have anything less than a wonderful time. I explore new fields or barnyards. Interesting plants grow around the cow pats, migrating birds swoop through the sky, chickens murmur and cluck. Even on the windiest autumn day, the work warms me. I make friends; it seems as though only kind people keep family cows. They tell me when the cow will calve and invite me to bring my children to see it. At the chicken farm I express my appreciation to the farmer—who has yet to charge me more than one dollar per garbage can—by buying a fat hen to take home for dinner.

In communities where cows and chickens are scarce, riding stables can sometimes be found with which gardeners might cultivate a relationship. When there are neither horses nor farm animals within reach, one can use bagged dried cow manure, which will still add nitrogen, though not in as lively a way as fresh manure that composts with the other ingredients. Blood meal, cottonseed meal, and fish meal are other packaged products that will help the nitrogen-carbon balance in the compost pile.

It matters where these substances originate. Cottonseed meal from cotton that had been saturated with chemicals would harm a compost pile: most insecticides do not discriminate between organisms that eat crops and those that create humus. And it would be better, for biological as well as moral reasons, not to use the manure of animals that never graze but are kept in feed lots. Therefore companies that have been developed to cater exclusively to organic farmers and gardeners are the best sources for compost additives that one cannot personally investigate (see Readings and Resources).

MINERALS AND TRACE ELEMENTS

Besides supplying animal products and fish meals, enlightened mail-order suppliers and local garden centers also offer a selection of mineral amendments in natural forms: rock phosphate, greensand, bone meal. After some study (see also chapter 2), gardeners might consider adding some of these to their compost piles. Some gardeners might add a variety of amendments, just to make sure their plants will get enough of everything. Other gardeners who suspect (because of symptoms in their plants or a soil test) a particular deficiency in the soil will look for whatever is needed to correct it.

As was pointed out in chapter 2, using soil amendments even in natural forms is something that must be done sparingly. There is always the risk that in trying to adjust one imbalance, one will end by creating another. But one of the marvels of the composting process is that it can balance out excess, and the same organisms that create humus from dying vegetable matter also transform relatively lifeless minerals into forms the plants can absorb. So if gardeners want to explore soil amendments the best way to do so is by adding them to the compost pile.

Bone meal is a good source of phosphorus, which stimulates flowering, as are rock phosphate (actually the tiny skeletons of prehistoric animals) and colloidal phosphate, which helps the soil structure of sandy gardens. Potassium makes strong roots, and greensand, a remnant of ancient seabeds, helps supply it. The mineral most commonly added to compost heaps is lime. One reason is that lime is an agent that "sweetens" an acid soil. But even gardeners whose soil is not acid will sometimes use lime for its calcium, which plays an important part in transforming raw plant materials into the humus that the plant can absorb. (I sprinkle a little lime into my big leaf pile to help it break down.) Lime must be handled carefully: it should not be put in direct contact with manure, or a nasty reaction will ensue, and one should avoid slaked or hydrated lime, which will burn the soil and plants. One of the gentlest, and therefore safest, forms of lime to use is pulverized oystershell.

Whether or not gardeners include these bagged products in their compost piles will depend a bit on their temperaments and a lot on where they live. City gardeners who do not have access to a great variety of raw materials may find such amendments a blessing and might rather enjoy bringing, say, prehistoric sea creatures or bat guano to their gardens. Country gardeners who are more likely to encounter heaps of spoilt hay, clumps of nettle, chicken manure, or tide wracks of seaweed and starfish may prefer to do their own foraging. Casting a wide net is a good way to make sure that the compost will provide all known nutrients, perhaps some unknown ones as well.

In either case, science should always be mixed with intuition in the compost heap. The surest way to achieve balance is through variety. This is the value of the kitchen bucket. Even if quantities are tiny, half a mushroom or some chamomile tea bags might provide the necessary trace of some vital element, or strand in the web of being.

FRESH GREENS

Close to compost day, one scours the garden one more time for whatever is green: weeds and aging annuals, grass clippings. The hunt should encompass not just what grows in the beds, but the patches of burdock behind the shed, the nettle patch under the apple tree, ground ivy and wild garlic in the shrub borders—whatever was previously invisible or a nuisance. Anything that is still fresh when it goes in the pile brings lively nitrogen and aids quick decomposition. Unless one has been much too tidy, a last-minute search through the wilder reaches of the garden will usually yield several wheelbarrows of just what one needs.

Building the pile

Although I would like now to proceed to building the pile, one of my favorite moments in the gardening year, I should in fairness point out that not every gardener *builds* a compost pile. There are other ways to consider.

Some gardeners simply pile everything up as it comes. Left to itself, the resulting heap gradually molders, becoming black and powdery at the bottom, while new green matter—apple cores, weeds—continue to be added at the top. The cool decay that takes place in such a pile will provide the garden with some organic matter good for mulching (although any weed seeds in the pile will sprout where they are spread). In a forest or wild garden, such a substance would be enough to close the cycle, but in a cultivated garden in which many different plants are growing and from which plants are continually being removed, it is not enough to nourish the garden. Sooner or later it will need something else. In some places one can buy serious quantities of already composted horse or cow manure; this and the mulch together would be likely to meet a garden's needs.

A richer compost is made when gardeners layer their heap as it accumulates. They might, for example, keep a pile of topsoil or some manure near their stockpile and with each barrowful of garden debris throw on a shovelful, perhaps even sprinkle on some rock dusts now and then. If they come across some treasures, a bucket or two of pond-bottom, a sack of seaweed, they mix it through with a pitchfork. If the pile begins to dry out, they water it, or if it looks too wet, they turn it with a fork. Usually the pile will heat up from time to time, indicating microorganisms hard at work making humus; if it is hot enough, the weed seeds will also be killed. This technique seems to work best when gardeners leave the pile alone for a few weeks or months (meanwhile beginning another one) before they use it, but some gardeners mine the bottom while adding to the top.

I have seen this kind of compost turn out very well and lovely gardens ensue. But on the whole this method is only reliable in cases where the gardeners have a strong grasp of what they are doing, manage to keep track of what went in and what did not, and monitor progress with an experienced eye. Usually such gardeners are hard-pressed to describe what they do. This is existential, improvisational compost-making, somewhat different every time—a technique that calls both for seizing the moment, weather, and material at hand, and for a strong individual sense of what the garden needs.

Both new gardeners and old ones who really want to depend on their compost will, I think, find success and even delight in composing their pile: first collecting what will go into it, then "making" the pile all at once. This takes a certain focus but not very much time, perhaps half a day once or twice a year. From the gardener's point of view, building the pile is a moment to really penetrate the composting process, a time when it becomes at once mysterious and clear.

While nothing is ever certain in a garden, the compost that ensues from this conscious composing is more likely to be truly active and to give the plants just what they need. The reason for this is that when decay happens gradually much of the vitality of the organic matter is dissipated, into the atmosphere and into mineralization. One assembles a pile to make sure all the substances are there, but also, in a sense, to ignite it—to initiate a continuous process wherein, as in an alchemist's crucible, breaking down and building up are one. A compost heap's warmth, so reassuring to the touch, is generated by thermophilic (heat-loving) bacteria at work breaking down leaves and bones into their elements, which—before they can dissipate into lifelessness—are quickly reconstituted by certain fungi into the great designs of molecules that constitute new life. If this happens quickly, nothing is lost and something new and rich is gained.

Compost day

The day arrives. Sometimes I have planned it, written its date on the calendar; other times I just wake up and smell moisture and liveliness, or hear excited birds, and decide there and then. I dress in my oldest, most comfortable clothes and start early.

The first step is to wheelbarrow everything to the site of the new pile: the accumulated garden and kitchen refuse, some of it already blackened by partial rotting, the newly gleaned green weeds and grass clippings, crimson and gold fallen leaves if it is autumn. Nearby is the manure (which usually comes from the farm with plenty of straw bedding mixed in), a bag of oystershell lime, and a quarter of a bucket of ash from the woodstove (good source of potassium if used in moderation). I fetch the pitchfork and spade and, if it is not raining, I get the hose ready.

Taking up my spade I mark out the edges of what will be the base of the heap. The size is always something of a guess, as it is difficult to know at the beginning exactly how things will end. I usually begin with a rectangle of about four feet by five. I know that the pile must be at least four by four feet at the bottom and should rise to three or four feet, the sides gradually sloping so that the pile becomes only about a foot and a half wide at the top.

The pile should sit on bare earth. Many of the soil creatures that will decompose the pile come from below. If there is grass, one needs to dig it out, setting the sod to one side to use later in the pile. Even if the earth is already bare, it is a good scheme to skim off an inch or two of soil and put it to one side to intersperse in the heap as it is built. The best base on which to build a new compost heap is where the old one once stood: the earth beneath it will be crawling with life. Of course there must always be a first time, and plain earth will also work.*

Then it begins. Everything that goes onto the pile must be wet. This is why, whenever possible, I make compost in the rain. I wear an old hooded camping raincoat and high rubber boots and get to work with the pitchfork. Not everyone enjoys rain as much as I do; if this method is not appealing or if there is no rain, one needs to use the hose, with a fine nozzle, to lightly spray each layer as it goes on.

The first layer to be forked onto the soil, or old compost, base should be two or three inches of the freshest green leaves and grasses. This is followed by a little soil or old compost. Then comes a thin layer of manure or blood meal—whatever is one's richest nitrogen source—followed by some of the older, more carbony garden pile, with maybe a handful of rock dust sprinkled on, or some wood ash. Any mineral additions should be added

---

*Plain earth might not work if one is making compost for the first time in a place where a lot of chemical fertilizers, insecticides, or weed killers have been used. Then the whole environment may have become so lifeless that nothing is left to start the pile. A compost starter—essentially soil inoculated with bacteria—might then be needed. There are many commercial products, but I recommend "Dr. Pfeiffer's bio-dynamic compost starter" from the Josephine Porter Institute as a reliable antidote to whatever is sterile and moribund.

with a light hand here and there, like herbs in the soup, but lime should be kept from direct contact with the manure.

Then one repeats the sequence, over and again: the green leaves with a little soil, the manure, the older garden stuffs, dustings of minerals. All this layering is to prevent too much concentration of any one ingredient, which slows down decomposition. Autumn leaves, for instance, piled by themselves will remain leaves for months and months, but they will crumble nicely if they are well distributed in the heap and dampened.

As the pile grows, one keeps an eye on the balance between water and air. When compost piles do not heat up at all, this is very often because they are too dry; many composting organisms need water to become active. On the other hand, the kind of rotting that ends in good compost requires the presence of oxygen. Airless decomposition results in putrefaction, which produces a cold, slimy, essentially worthless substance. This is what happens if the pile is so saturated with water that it drives out air. The rule of thumb is that anywhere in the pile that one puts one's hand should feel damp, but never so wet that, when squeezed, water runs out.

Working like this, it can take half a day to build a pile. Perhaps one cannot set aside so much time all at once, or perhaps there is time, but one's arms and shoulders begin to ache; or one might run out of a certain ingredient and decide to go and rake or search for more. It is quite all right to take breaks. The pile need not be built in a day; though it is good if it can be finished within a week, so that everything decomposes together.

Another biodynamic refinement

When the pile is about half built, I pause and make six holes with my rake handle. In each of these I bury one of the six biodynamic compost preparations, made respectively of yarrow, chamomile, nettle, oak bark, dandelion, and valerian (some of the valerian is kept back and sprayed over the finished pile). This is a refinement and is entirely optional, but I always put them in, feeling that if I have gone to the trouble of building the pile, I might as well truly organize it.

The quantities of these preparations that go into even a large compost pile are tiny: a teaspoon of each dark powder, a milliliter of expressed juice of valerian flowers. As with the horn manure spray (see chapter 2), using them in the garden is not a matter of adding substances, but of setting processes in motion—rather as homeopathic medicines stimulate activity in the body. Though they are used together as a set, each of the six preparations works according to its own particular plant nature, each relating to specific elemental processes: yarrow, for example, to sulfur and potassium metabolism, dandelion to silica. The purpose of adding them to the pile in process is to make a compost that is more responsive and will render the soil more "intelligent," sharpening its receptivity to the larger environment and allowing the plants to find what they need.

I watched these preparations being made around our house and garden many times when my former husband made them for his farm. I know how precisely they must be assembled and with what careful consideration of the plant part to be used—leaf, blossom, bark—the moment in its life (the flower perhaps just opening but not full) and of the year when it is picked, where it must be stored and for how long, and the peculiar concoctions that ensue if a single step goes wrong. Now I gratefully order them ready-made from the Josephine Porter Institute, with a proper reverence for their dark substantiality.

Most organic gardeners make good compost without using biodynamic preparations. Those that do use them have either read about them in the lectures of Rudolf Steiner or in pamphlets by Ehrenfried Pfeiffer, which so vividly evoke the nature of the plants used in the preparations and of the animal sheaths that contain them that the function of each one in the garden becomes almost palpable. Either that, or they have been swayed by some garden where the compost looked particularly black and lively, the plants vital, and where the gardener adds them to the heap. The latter is a more common inspiration than the former, since neither Steiner nor Pfeiffer is easy to read. It was my fate to fall into both categories, to have read the writings and to have been moved by the gardens. Every year I particularly look forward to the moment when I pause halfway through building the pile to consider the subtle forces at work.

Finishing touches

When at last one comes to the end of building, because there is nothing left with which to build, the top of the heap should be flattened with the back of the spade till its profile resembles an ancient mountain. This is to catch rain and keep the pile moist. If the heap seems too loosely strewn and airy, I climb on top and gently tread it down. Or if it feels too dense and compacted (too little air), I loosen the layers a little with the fork.

The whole heap should then be covered with a light "skin," which shelters it even as it allows air and moisture to come in. I use sod (with the grass turned inward), or straw, or damp leaves. It depends on what I can get. The purpose of this covering is to insulate and contain the heap, leaving it to its powerful inner workings. Now it is an entity.

The next stage for gardeners must be something like what potters experience when, having done all they can to shape and glaze the pots, they put them in the kiln for the heat to effect its transformations. The process is now largely out of their hands, but they watch just the same, peeping through a hole and making small adjustments with the controls that remain.

A finished heap may become active within a day or two, or it may take a week, especially if the days are cold. The sign that a compost heap has begun to work is heat, not just any heat but a particular, living heat, distinctly warm, but not too hot. Gardeners who feel happier with a definitive number can use a compost thermometer; the temperature should be within 10 degrees of 120 (all temperatures are Fahrenheit). Without a thermometer, one can make a little hole about halfway up the pile and feel a foot deep for a heat that will warm a bare hand, but is not so hot that one has to quickly pull it out again.

If everything has gone right, this heat just comes. But with so many variables, matters do not always go smoothly. Then gardeners, like Prospero on his island, must work the elements—juggle a little with earth, fire, and water till they cohere. If, when one feels into a test hole, the compost stays cold, the question becomes: what kind of cold: wet and slimy, or dry and flaky? If it is the latter, then one finds a tool that can poke holes well into the pile. A crowbar is good for this, and so is a special tool called a compost aerator (rather like a crowbar with a collapsible propeller at the end); or I have managed with a rake handle. Having made a number of holes in the sides and top, one pours in water with the hose. Doing this for a few minutes every day will dampen the pile enough to start it going. If, on the other hand, the pile feels cold but wet, one makes the same kinds of holes, but in this case it is just to let in air. The compost aerator device with the propeller is particularly good for this.

A sign of too much heat is steam rising from the top of the pile. One need not worry if steam rises from the test holes: the center of the pile is always much warmer than the periphery, but the surface should not be quite so hot. Water will cool a hot pile just as it can heat a cold one. Once again the remedy is to make holes and pour in water, and one could lightly hose the outside as well.

More often than not, the heap gets to work without any meddling at all. Still, I always wait and worry, watching the pile as it crouches like a sleeping animal in its skin of frost-laced straw. Then the morning comes when, reaching in my hand, I feel the sudden warmth where yesterday was only the clammy cold of the piled-up corpses of everything in the garden that has died. Out of that heat will issue the rose and the parsley and the carrots, the bees, the white narcissus, and jasmine scent on summer evenings.

Serial transformation

At this stage the gardener's work is almost done, but the work of the soil creatures is only beginning. After the drama of heat generated by the transformations of the thermophilic bacteria, the compost gradually cools (to know just when this is, the inquisitive gardener can keep making holes and feeling with a hand, taking care each time to close them again) and the worms and actinomycetes come in and begin their silent operations. These are the creatures that through the substances and processes of their own organisms create humus. This phase takes longer.

If the weather is warm it may be three months before the compost is ready to use; perhaps six months if one is composting over winter. The way to tell is by the scent. Humus smells as one might imagine it would: like green growth itself, or like rain, earthy and sweet. It will still have some lumps in it, but they are connected only by threads and crumble quickly, and the worms will still be present.

This is the best time to use compost: the stage at which it is most lively. If it is spring, one very carefully and gently (so as not to root out any plants that might still be underground) scratches around the perennials and shrubs, taking out weeds and old leaves and preparing a surface, no longer caked and dull, but stirred and receptive. Then one scatters the compost in wide circles around the crowns of the plants. Or, if one has made new beds, one loads up the wheelbarrow and shovels a layer several inches thick of the moist, tendrilous compost on every bit of bare earth one can reach, leaving it on the surface for the worms to carry down or scratching it in a little with a tined cultivator.

I never have quite enough compost. Either I use up the whole pile in spring planting and top-dressing and then have none to use for summer mulching and fall planting, or I use the pile abstemiously and do have enough for summer and fall, but feel I have been mean. Some years, I make extraordinary efforts and make a spring pile as well as an autumn pile, and then there is plenty.

Other years I do not manage to make compost at all and the heaps of debris just crumble away to not very much. And twice disaster struck in the form of northeasterly storms at equinoctial tides and the compost heaps washed out to sea, were gone; who knows where?

Chapter 4

Beginning from Seed

... He has seen the light lie down
in the dung heap, and rise again in the corn.
His thought passes along the row ends like a mole.
What miraculous seed has he swallowed
that the unending sentence of his love flows out of his mouth
like a vine clinging in the sunlight, and like water
descending in the dark?

> Wendell Berry, "The Man Born to Farming"

Seeds are the archetypal beginning, the unit of being. Sometimes they are so small one can hardly see them. A tomato seed may be mistaken for a speck of dust, but a gardener drops it carefully into soil and covers it up, knowing that within that speck lies the whole story of first leaves, thickening stem, pale yellow flowers, fruit ripening green to scarlet, sweet tomato scent wafting through the summer air. There are other ways to bring plants into the garden: digging in bulbs and tubers, cuttings and divisions, whole rooted plants. Gardeners choose which way depending on the plant (is it a carrot or a rose?) and the temperament of the gardener, and may not sow seeds very often. But I know of no garden work that goes so straight to the heart of the matter as planting a seed, so seeds are a good place to start.

The ability to start seeds successfully varies from gardener to gardener and does not always tally with good results in other aspects of working with plants. One gardener I know, whose garden has the green loveliness that comes only from good health, surprised me when he confessed that he hardly starts any plants from seed: "I'm just not good at it; perhaps I'm too young." Another friend, not old, never visits my garden without taking away a seedpod or two of something he has noticed. He seems to know exactly when to drop in and carries a sharp knife and an envelope in his pocket. By now just about anything beautiful or rare that is growing in my garden is also growing in his, my tastiest pole bean, a shell-pink cyclamen (which took him four years to grow into flower). While he is not in other ways an extraordinary gardener, he is probably a soul mate of the person who sprouted the four-thousand-year-old lotus seeds found in an Egyptian pyramid.

My own beginning with seeds was not auspicious. I had many failures. I attributed these to a lack of greenness in myself and felt sad and a bit ashamed. Over the years, however, I have become much better at it. Though I am still amazed to see each tiny cotyledon, my seeds are much more likely to sprout than not. Success with germinating seeds is a question of orderliness and precision, steadiness of hand and eye, patience, trust, perseverance. Some gardeners come by these qualities naturally; others, like myself, must struggle their whole lives to develop them.

Seeds for beginners

For evolutionary reasons, there is a wide range of sensitivity in the plant world. Some seeds are demanding and idiosyncratic. To reach the point of germination they require warmth and deep cold and warmth again in a very particular sequence, or else they need a specific length of day or night, must lie exposed on top of the soil, or else be deeply buried. Others are much more tolerant and will sprout almost anywhere given the slightest encouragement. These are the ones with which to try one's hand.

Calendula seeds are friendly to gardeners. They germinate outside quickly and reliably in many sorts of weather. They are just big enough so that a single seed can be held between two fingers and placed exactly where one wants. They are big enough, too, that the naked eye can take in their intriguing form and texture: little crescents, striated within the curve and bumpy down the back, with a minute horn at each end.

Beyond their helpful qualities as seeds, calendulas grow into plants that bring sun colors to the flower and vegetable beds and blossom for a long time, defying the frost when other flowers have long gone. Their English name is pot marigold, and some people eat the flower petals in salads. Here they will be grown as exemplars.

I choose a spring day when the soil is neither wet nor dusty dry, and when it is unlikely there will be another frost. I will plant the calendulas at one end of a sunny garden bed dug over and compost-covered two weeks earlier. The soil looks moist, lumpy, and ready, but seeds need a smooth, level bed for their tiny roots to take hold. So I gently comb the surface with a metal straight rake, taking out any pebbles or twigs as I go, disturbing invisible weeds.

I intend to plant all the seeds in my packet, about forty. When fully grown each plant will need almost a square foot of space. But in considering how to space the seeds, I must keep in mind that probably not all will come up, and also that I am going to transplant at least half of those that do. (Calendulas are easy to move and nice to have on hand to fill empty spaces among vegetables or to illuminate dark corners of a flower bed.) Having drawn lines in the soil with a finger, I place the seeds—pressing each one firmly down in staggered rows with about four inches between seeds and four inches between rows. In the end there will be a patch of plants in a kind of honeycomb pattern.

The general rule for covering seeds (there are exceptions, including some seeds that should not be covered at all) is twice the depth of their own thickness. I crumble the soil carefully between my fingers so that no heavy clod will bury a seed. Then, very gently, I tap the soil lightly down with the palms of my hands, the way one might tuck in a baby, securing the seeds in their bed.

I hope for a gentle rain to wake them, or even a heavy shower, though a few seeds might get knocked out of place. But by the following morning, no rain has come, so I water the seeds myself, using a watering can with a rose that pours out little rainlike drops. A hose with a fine nozzle would also work, but one must always be careful not to turn the tap on too hard. Once they are watered, the seeds are on their way and cannot be allowed to dry out lest the new shoots shrivel and die.*

Then the waiting begins. Some packets or seed catalogues give an indication of how long the seeds may take to germinate. This is helpful but approximate. Seeds germinate in direct relation to

---

*There are no rules about how often to water a seedbed in order to keep it moist. Every soil is different. After a while, gardeners come to know their own soil and weather and can guess. But at the beginning it is a good idea to make a habit of feeling the soil for moisture an inch or two below the surface every rainless day.

temperature, sprouting faster the warmer the soil is, until it gets too hot and they will not germinate at all. If the soil stays cold, the seeds will take their time, and wait where they are even for weeks and months. Moon, stars, and eclipses will also play their part, sometimes accounting for swift bursts and mysterious lags.

Occasionally the seeds do not come up at all. Perhaps a cat scratched them out, or a bird ate them, or a mole tunneled straight through, or sometimes, very rarely, one gets a bad lot. One seldom finds out what really happened, but should not despair too soon. Terse, haikulike notes in a garden cal- endar are valuable here: "March 23rd dug out dead rose, planted peas, saw robin, at night it snowed." If the diary has moon and star positions (see chapter 12 on *Stella Natura* planting calendar), these will provide additional clues. What seems a very long time might turn out to have been only three weeks, and the seeds could still sprout.

For nine days after planting the calendula seeds, there is noth- ing to see. Then the first cotyledon appears, radiant apple green against black soil. Cotyledons are the "seed leaves" that precede the true leaves, and often resemble the shape of the seed. They can be very tiny, so one might not see them at first, unless one goes out every day and stares at the earth, which is something I often find myself doing while still half awake on pale spring mornings. On the eleventh day two more straggle out. Then on the first really warm day all the others suddenly assemble in a crowd.

Over the next two months I watch as the plants develop their first leaves, one pair rising out of the other, then stems and side branches. At midsummer the leaves grow smaller and spiral in toward the stem to make the first flower buds. All summer the tight green buds form and round and open into flower discs, burnt orange and sun yellow. Then as the petals drop, the new sickle-shaped horned green seeds appear. They ripen into brown, and it all begins again.

More challenging seeds

Among the annual flowers, cosmos, cornflowers, and sunflowers are also good for seed practice, as are beans and spinach in the vegetable garden. They all germinate quickly when the soil is warm (spinach actually prefers it cool) and have big enough seeds so that one can see and feel what one is doing.

Tiny seeds, like lettuce or carrots or larkspur, need more dexterity. Weightless and almost invisible against the soil, they are difficult to plant without clumping them too closely together. Some gardeners mix the seed with a little sand to achieve a better distribution. They must be covered with the thinnest possible layer of fine soil. I take very small pinches of seed and scatter them as widely as I can on a windless day. The plants still come up too close together, but I can manage this by thinning.

Some gardeners have trouble with thinning. They are so grateful for each sprouting shoot that it pains them to pull any out. I had this difficulty myself, until experience taught me to overcome such feelings for the sake of the plants. Failure to thin decisively is the most common cause of spindly plants that never become what they could. Each individual needs its proper space and air, usually more than one thinks.

Thinning is an ongoing process; one does it little by little as the plants grow and leaves or roots begin to intrude upon one another. As with the calendulas, some of the thinned plants can be transplanted into other beds with a sharp, narrow trowel, but usually not all. If one eats the thinnings in soups or salads, or composts them in the pile, their short lives are not wasted.

Seeds that take a very long time to germinate present other challenges. Seeds of many perennial flowers and herbs are like this, and even a few annuals. They take so long that one tends to forget they are there, in which case they might dry out or be overcome by weeds. Another pitfall is that the soil above them can become crusted, making it difficult for the first shoots to get through. If one plants such seeds accompanied by those of a plant that germinates and grows very fast—perhaps radishes or white turnips—then the growth of the quickly sprouting plants keeps the soil from baking and also holds one's attention. The radishes and turnips will be ready to harvest before they begin to crowd the later-emerging plants.

Certain seeds, especially of perennials, have minds of their own. More than once I have sown seeds in spring, seen no sign of life, given up, and then been surprised to see little plants the following year, or even the year after that, when they seem to have determined that conditions were more auspicious for coming into being.

Seeds of adventure and memory

Starting plants from seed may seem slow and plodding, sometimes frustrating, but it is at the same time a most adventurous way to garden. One has only to consider the immense possibilities that stem from these small beginnings.

The range of seed companies that will send seeds and catalogues to one's door is astonishingly wide. The famous Hudson's Ethnobotanical Catalogue "dedicated to the distribution of seeds and knowledge" opens the whole world to a gardener. Hudson's range includes *Primula veris* seeds, the dainty English cowslip that I wanted for years, and *Adansonia digitata,* the African baobab tree, whose trunk can grow to thirty feet in circumference and whose leaves are eaten like spinach: "Hollowed out: they are used as rooms. Worshipped as fertility tree" (three dollars a packet). Hudson points out:

> We offer many seeds which are easy, and sprout quickly and evenly. But with some you must be prepared to experiment, be patient, exercise initiative & intuition, remembering that with some rare species you are venturing into unknown territory. Most corporate seed companies will not carry difficult seeds, only selling easy, mass-produced varieties. We like to offer a more challenging alternative.

The baobab tree probably falls into the "challenging" category, and it would not grow on Long Island. But cowslips do, and Hudson's offers excellent cultural directions on starting the whole range of their seeds, including tropical ones, tree seeds, and other seeds requiring special treatment, all with the clear goal: not the company's financial profit, but the encouragement of gardeners to keep plant diversity alive.

For enthusiasts of one plant or another there are companies that specialize only in primulas, in chilies, in flowers that attract hummingbirds. Seeds allow one to track down and grow the exact varieties one wants, and this opportunity is available at prices of seldom more than a few dollars a packet. Seeds of

Change, as well as a number of locally based firms, specializes in heirloom varieties of vegetables, herbs, and flowers, tried-and-true varieties (also true-to-type, which means that once grown out, they will grow again from their own seeds) that have been kept alive by seed-saving gardeners for some special characteristic. Like Hudson's these companies encourage gardeners to preserve a multiplicity of vanishing varieties. This consideration is not at all nostalgic—though it may sound so at first—but profoundly practical and future-oriented. From the perspective of the garden, being able to choose from a range of idiosyncratic varieties allows gardeners to track down and grow the plants that do well where they live. From a global perspective there is the concern that as large corporate seed companies get bigger and bigger, they grow fewer and fewer varieties, raising the specter not only of monotony in gardens, but of worldwide crop failures. It has happened in the past, and not just in Eden, that the seeds of the future came out of a garden; it may happen again.

Finding and saving seeds

Then there are the seeds that one does not buy, but that once one starts noticing, begin to fall to one's hand: off one's own plants, in neighbors' gardens, in woods, meadows, and marshes at home or anywhere in the world. Every year I plant seeds of a pretty mallow, almost the same as, but a slightly deeper, warmer pink than, the Silver Cup one can buy. I grow this one because it came from two saucer-shaped pods I picked off a little plant that caught my eye as it lifted its flowers to the sun on a certain Swiss hillside. I had traveled a long way to that place; and then could spend only a few hours. Now I grow the mallows every year and revisit it.

Sometimes seeds come in letters from friends far away: "Here is that poppy you liked last summer," "White Maltese Cross, don't plant it near the crimson ones, they mix and get ugly. How are you doing, anyway?" The flowers that grow from them are companionable when one is lonely.

A woman in my village has a garden made almost entirely of local wildflowers and shrubs, which she grows both because she loves them and for the warblers and finches, dragonflies and butterflies they attract. A serious conservationist, she would never dig up a wild plant. Instead she collects seeds in the field, always being careful to leave the plant with many more pods remaining than she has taken away. Her success is largely due to timing and replication. She only picks the seeds when they are at their ripest, just about to burst out of the pods, and she plants them at the same time they would drop in nature and in similar situations, rocky or moist, sunny or shady, to those in which she has seen them thriving in the wild.

Choosing the right moment to harvest is also crucial in saving seeds from one's own garden plants. One does not want to miss them, but they have to be ripe. Once they have been gathered, husks or pods must be gently removed and the seeds dried in the air, spread out on a tray. They should be kept dry and stored in closed glass jars away from light in a cool, not freezing, place. Seeds should be gathered only from the healthiest, most beautiful specimens, so it is wise to mark one's seed plants early and to keep an eye on them. Doing this year after year will produce a strain that is especially well adapted to one's own garden.

Seed-saving only works if the plant from which one gathers seed is open-pollinated and not a hybrid, since the latter cannot reproduce true to type, whereas the former does. One may also get strange results if the plant is the type that cross-pollinates with other plants in the same family. For years I wondered why it often happens that a single acorn squash that looks exactly like its sweet-tasting neighbors can taste so nasty. A seed collector told me that its particular parent or grandparent might have crossed with pollen from a gourd growing within bee-flying distance, with bitter results.

Seed catalogues will tell if a particular variety is hybrid or open-pollinated. A sure sign of a good seed to save is one from a plant that has already been volunteering successfully in one's garden. To be sure about which plants are self-pollinating and which ones cross-pollinate with what, and of how far apart to plant different vegetables to avoid such crossing, one needs a good reference book. Such a book will also tell which seeds need special treatment, like exposure to freezing temperatures or to light, during their dormancy. Johnny's Seeds sells an excellent informative basic manual, *Growing Garden Seeds,* which makes a good beginning. Beyond that Suzanne Ashworth's *Seed to Seed* is packed with highly specific, invaluable information for serious seed savers. But even without a book, or when the plant in question is not listed (or one does not even know what it is), one can go a long way on impulse and observation.

Seeds in winter

In winter when it is quiet, I sometimes find myself sifting through my seeds, maybe checking the jars and packets for dampness or beetles, but really just having a look. I might take out half a dozen—maybe a bush bean seed, parsley, a cornflower, mustard, cosmos, corn—and set them on the table in front of me. I ponder how different each is from the other and how finely each is articulated. Choosing just one, I trace in my mind's eye, with all the precision I can muster, what, step by step, it will become.

Besides allowing such moments of contemplation, winter may also lead gardeners to the perplexing question of whether or not to start seeds indoors. Gardeners who live where winters are mild can plant annuals in autumn or early spring and never need to start seeds indoors, unless they have seeds of something rare or fragile they want to protect. Those who live in those extreme northern or mountainous regions where July is the only sure frost-free month must shelter so many seedlings that building a greenhouse or cold frame is often the only practical way to proceed. All others must decide if and how to integrate trays of plants into their lives and households during long winters and uncertain springs.

People and plants ought to be able to live together more easily than they usually do. It is a pity that the passive solar houses of the 1970s with built-in heat-storing greenhouses did not become the standard for the twentieth century. Perhaps they will in the twenty-first. Like many gardeners, I would love a greenhouse. Any gardener who lives in a house like mine—old, cold, dusty, and dark, its few sunny windowsills already claimed by children and cats—is doomed to frustration if he or she believes, as I once did, that most of their vegetable seeds can be planted indoors. Certainly it *can* be done, but I have concluded it may be better to wrestle with the elements than with one's own family.

In dim, unruly households it might not only be the gardeners but also the plants that do better taking their chances outside. Gardeners, unlike farmers, can work with calculated risk. Seeds can often be planted outside earlier than the packet suggests, as long as the ground can be worked. It is true some seedlings might be lost, but usually not many, and one can often try again. If one sees or feels a frosty night coming—no wind, bite in the air, bright stars—one can save the situation by covering the most vulnerable plants with a plastic tarpaulin or a blanket. (I have not gone so far as to use plastic row tunnels and other fabricated devices, but if I lived a little farther north, I would.) The plants that do survive an early sowing are usually well-rooted and have a constitutional advantage over those that have suffered the shock of transplanting.

Planting the fast-growing varieties offered in seed catalogues is another way to avoid indoor starts. I can plant leeks outside and they will grow to full size by fall if they are King Richard (75 days), but not if they are Blue Solaise (105 days).

True warm-weather plants like tomatoes and peppers, or tender annual flowers like impatiens and petunia, will not stand frost at all, nor will they grow well if they are exposed to temperatures just above it. But if one does not want very many of these, it can be more sensible to go and buy plants after the last frost. These days many organic farmers sell their extra greenhouse plants at farm stands. This makes it easy to mix varieties: some early-ripening tomatoes, some late, and to grow just three eggplants and a pepper or two. I do not buy many tender annual flower plants because I mostly plant the hardy ones: cornflowers, calendulas, larkspur, which I can sow outside in April and like better anyway. Perhaps this is taste accommodating to situation, but that too is gardening.

A few seeds indoors

I have elaborated on how to avoid starting seeds indoors because many gardeners are made miserable by trying to do too much. However, it would be a shame if the pitfalls of excess kept anyone from the joys of doing a little. Once a gardener is freed from the sense of iron necessity and chore, he or she might discover that a flat or two of sprouting seeds around the house is a source of delight, even insight, as well as of little plants.

One could just start seeds of plants that would be difficult or expensive to grow any other way—a rare pepper variety, enough long-spurred columbines or bellflowers to make a cloud of them. Or one might take another tack and grow something fast and simple, lettuce perhaps, to thrill a child.

A sunny windowsill, if one has even one, will usually work as well and be far more beautiful to watch in the changing light of day than a special stand with fluorescent lights suspended over it. Almost unlimited technology exists for starting seeds indoors. Gardeners who really need it will find it easily enough, but too much paraphernalia is a burden.

Certain simple, well-designed pieces of equipment, on the other hand, can avert predictable mistakes. Many good seed companies (with a stake in a gardener's success) sell these items for a few dollars. Plastic trays allow one to water the flats without spoiling the windowsills. Flats with little drainage holes and individual cells help space the plants correctly, and clear acrylic covers hold moisture and warmth in and keep babies and cats out. It is a lot of plastic, but one can wash these items and use them year after year.

Starting mixtures can be made out of garden soil combined with leaf mold and sand or moss. A soil in which to start seeds is not primarily to nourish the plants (for the first weeks seedlings live on their own stored food), but it should be a substance that is free of weed seeds and fungus and is light yet able to hold moisture well. Garden soil should therefore be moistened, then sterilized in the oven (for about an hour at 250 degrees: it will smell very nasty) lest green molds attack vulnerable seedlings. The proportions of sand or moss must be adjusted to the particular soil to prevent the soil from caking in the flats. To make a mix that works requires experiment and can take on a fascination of its own. But many serious growers, as well as home gardeners, use commercial organic mixtures instead. These are sterile composts, already mixed with perlite and peat moss. They are also available from good seed companies and even some hardware stores and have been developed with care and thought.

Light and temperature matter most. One needs a windowsill facing south, or at least east. If it is not wide enough to hold a flat, one gets as close as one can with a table or piled-up boxes. A difficulty some people have, especially in old houses, is that windows can get very cold, especially at night. Here I admit to finding an electronic gadget very helpful. Plug-in rubber heating mats are available (also from seed catalogues) that go under the flats and keep the soil temperature at 70 degrees irrespective of the temperature of the air. These are expensive, but buying one is probably cheaper than trying to raise the temperature of the whole house and less wasteful.

The soil mixture should be moistened before it is put in the flats. After the seeds are planted, it should never be allowed to dry out completely. Neither should it be oversoaked, lest the seeds rot. Tepid water helps keep the soil warm. The acrylic lids maintain moisture in the flats, and now and then should be lifted off for ventilation.

Then one waits for a week, ten days, a month; sometimes two months and longer for perennial seeds. It depends on what one has planted and how warm the house is. Other rhythms also play a part, especially lunar cycles; often half a dozen seeds germinate after four weeks, then none at all, then in another month another half dozen appear, the next month still more. There could only be a tide at work.

Gardeners who wonder if all this could be worthwhile are changed once the first green shoot, seed coat still balanced on its head, unfolds into greenness. One becomes intimate with the seeds that sprout on one's windowsill, often while the snow is still on the ground, noticing each tiny node as it appears. At eye level the smallest lobes and swellings stand out. Metamorphosis speaks.

After germination plants still need to be kept inside for many weeks. As time goes on they may need to be fed; liquid kelp works well. If they outgrow their first flats, they will need transplanting into other flats—open trays without dividers—or eventually into small pots of their own. The very tender plants (like tomatoes) have to stay inside longest, and this can be a problem, causing the phenomenon of trays full of pale and leggy plants haunting the house because it is still too cold to go outside. This can only be avoided through careful research into one's earliest expected frost-free date and the growth rate of the particular plant. It is better to start seeds of tender plants a little too late than a little too early.

Toward planting time gardeners begin the process called hardening off, setting the plants outside in their containers, and bringing them in at night at first if the weather is still unsettled. These ventures into nature accustom the plants to the open air before the shock of transplanting.

A lot can go wrong with tiny seedlings, and there is only so much one can do to protect them. While typing this chapter I set out a small tray of pretty green lettuces to sun themselves on my workroom doorstep. Within minutes a fat squirrel dropped out of an oak tree, sat down in the middle of the flat, and scratched. In the split second before I chased it back up the tree, it shredded half the lettuces I had nursed into being for ten weeks. Squatting on a flat is not what one would expect of a squirrel, but perhaps the unexpected is invited when one attempts such total control. Indoor seed-starting demands what is almost impossible: compulsive engagement joined to the ability to easily let go.

Chapter 5 Transplanting and Propagating

Watching hands transplanting,
Turning and tamping,
Lifting the young plants, with two fingers,
Sifting in a palm-full of fresh loam,—
One swift movement,—
Then plumping in the bunched roots,
A single thrust of the thumbs, a tamping and turning,
All in one,
Quick on the wooded bench,
A shaking down while the stem stays straight,
Once, twice, and a faint third thump,—
Into the flat-box it goes,
Ready for the long days under the sloped glass:

The sun warming the fine loam,
The young horns winding and unwinding,
Creaking their thin spines,
The underleaves, the smallest buds
Breaking into nakedness,
The blossoms extending
Out into the sweet air,
The whole flower extending outward,
Stretching and reaching.

Theodore Roethke, "Transplanting"

*P*lants find their ways into gardens by many other routes besides the slow and methodical process of growing from a carefully sown seed. Gardeners buy little plants in pots (or big ones with balled roots) from nurseries or garden centers. They are given them, wrapped in newspapers, by friends who have too many. They order bulbs and bare-roots from catalogues, or they propagate—by cutting or division—and make more plants out of those they already have. Some plants just show up, bird-planted, wind-scattered, or sprouting from a rhizome that crept underground from next door.

A dense network of relationship, of commerce, husbandry, and happenstance, underlies every garden. I think that when I wander through my garden, or work in it, the origin and history of each plant makes itself felt, whether I think of it or not. The leafy currant bushes with dangling shiny fruit and green wasps hovering nearby were once dry strikes—three-inch twigs—wrapped in a damp paper towel and nestled in my handbag as I flew home from a visit to a friend. The pale blue yellow-centered crocuses that ray out under the big oak each spring are descendants of a few corms planted very carefully by my oldest son—the one who recently spent a week in jail for defending a redwood forest—when he was six. Each story haunts the beds and borders, even as each plant it belongs to forms part of a new whole, the community that is the garden.

Transplanting—a gentle technique

Nature did not mean plants to move; roots want to take hold and stay. A seedling undergoing transplant shock is a poignant, desperate sight—every plant part withers and curls; the stem goes limp and lies flat on the ground. Yet setting out and transplanting has been part of gardening since Paradise. With good timing and attentiveness, a gardener can move almost any plant so gently that it sleeps through the whole experience, waking up cheerfully in a better place.

Whether one is taking a little seedling out of a flat, a plant from a pot, or transplanting a plant that is already growing in another part of one's garden, the concern is much the same: to disturb the roots as little as possible. Roots should not be torn or bumped or allowed to dry out. All these things can happen when a gardener is not careful.

To keep roots from harm each plant should be moved with as much soil around its roots as possible. In this way the plant travels from place to place wrapped in its familiar environment, remaining within it until it is confident enough to grow out into what lies beyond. Moisture is critical. If a plant is dug out of dry soil, the soil will fall away as soon as it is lifted, exposing the roots to sun and wind. Roots shrink from sun and wind. If the soil is damp, however, it will hold together, clinging to the roots in a little clod or a big lump.

The best way to transplant is to wait for a day when it has been raining recently, but the soil is not so very wet that it cannot be worked. It should be just about to rain again, the sky overcast, perhaps with distant thunder rumbling and the air full of green electricity. Wonders can be worked on days like this, and gardeners come to love them.

Sometimes it is not possible to wait for the right day. The seedlings might be crowding out of their flats, or one might have been given bare-rooted irises wrapped in a newspaper. Then the right weather must be imitated. An hour or two before planting, one dampens the soil in which one is going to plant and waters the plants, whether they are in pots or in the ground. If the day is blindingly bright and windy, it is best to wait till the afternoon shadows fall, so the plants can recover in the moist night air.

New holes should be made ready before the plants to be moved are dug out. A dibber—a small metal-pointed tool—is useful for making holes for a little seedling, or a narrow trowel will do, as long as one remembers that the idea is to make a hole without taking out any soil. But a hole for an already established plant must always be more than ample for its roots; the topsoil dug out and carefully piled to one side, and the soil at the bottom loosened with a digging fork. In a clay soil it is wise also to loosen up the sides of the hole so the roots are not presented with impenetrable walls.

Seedlings in a flat should not be pulled by the stem, but eased out with a spoon or small trowel. The best way to get a plant out of its pot is to hold it upside down, one hand flat against the soil, and to hit the pot's bottom with a trowel if the plant sticks. To move a plant already in the ground to a new home, one takes a sharp spade and digs a circle around the crown of the plant at a distance wide enough that one is unlikely to be cutting roots. If the soil is moist, it should be possible to lift out the root ball all in one lump. If it comes apart after all, one might find oneself with two plants instead of one, which is not always so bad.

The planting is done with a watering can nearby and a wheelbarrow full of screened compost or fine topsoil that roots will easily penetrate. One hand holds the plant erect, while the other gently surrounds its roots with compost. If the plant is a rootbound nursery plant (the roots tangled around themselves in a white mesh, climbing the walls of the pot), one might need to gently pull the roots apart and guide them into the surrounding soil. With only a few exceptions, the crown of the plant where root becomes stem should not be set higher than the grade of the soil. Having set the plant in place, one carefully refills the hole, then decisively firms down the soil around the crown with one's hands or bare feet. The plant craves secure anchorage, without air pockets that could starve a root.

As soon as it is in place, the plant needs to be soaked from the watering can. Watering, by the gardener or rain, has to be done at least twice a week, sometimes more often if it is windy, until the plant is "established." One gradually gets a sense for what this word means and how long it takes. A plant is not really at home until its roots have reached out beyond its original growing medium and connected the plant securely to its new place. Once this has occurred, it is much more able to fend for itself. Annuals will make the transition sooner than slow-growing perennials. Bushes and trees sometimes need a year. The bigger the plant the longer it needs watching, and extra water at drought times.

Timing and patience

Once one has begun to move plants around and seen them live, it can be tempting to go on and on, trying out new effects, making

a new garden every week. Usually this is an impulse to resist. Plants, unlike furniture, are not things, but beings with their own intentions to which attention must be paid. It is entirely possible to rearrange one's garden. Sooner or later everyone does, if only to keep it the same. But rearrangement needs to be implemented slowly, bit by bit, bending to the season of each plant. Meanwhile the picture of how the garden might someday appear waits patiently in the gardener's mind.

Annuals grow best if they are transplanted early in their lives and then left alone. It is even possible to move the difficult ones, like cornflowers, mallow, and cosmos, if it is early enough in the life of the plant (when only two or three leaf pairs have formed) and if one digs them up with big trowelfuls of damp soil around their roots.

When perennials are transplanted depends mostly on when they bloom. A plant that is focusing its whole being on preparing flowers should be left in peace. Otherwise the strain of moving can cause its flower buds to wither, or, worse, the whole plant might languish and never recover. When flowering is over, and especially if the flower stalks are cut off so as not to let the plant go to seed, the plant will put all its growing force into its roots. This is the best time to transplant, as long as the weather will allow it.

Perennials that bloom very early in spring can be moved as soon as they have finished flowering. One can also move those that flower in late spring or early summer after they have bloomed, as long as one waters them devotedly. If the summer will be extremely hot and dry, it is better to wait till early in the autumn. Autumn, since it is often moist and serene, can be the perfect time to remake a garden, but only if the autumn is long enough so that plants can grow roots for several weeks before a hard frost. This is why such late-flowering plants as chrysanthemums or Japanese anemones cannot be moved till spring (when they should be moved as soon as they appear).

Deciduous bushes and trees are best moved (either within the garden or from a nursery) in autumn when their leaves are just fallen, but again only if there will be enough time for them to settle in a little before temperatures go down steeply. If there will not be such a pause, or if the winter can be counted on to be extremely cold, it is better to wait for spring.

Even in springtime, gardeners transplanting trees and shrubs have to be on the alert. The earth should be completely thawed out, without lingering frozen clods, and the soil friable, crumbling easily in the hand. But leaf buds should still be furled, or only the least bit opened. Where I live, by the sea, the season is slow and forgiving. Even so, I often miss the moment and have to wait another year. Where springs come suddenly, gardeners must be poised for action.

Evergreens can be moved with a little more leeway. They can be planted a bit earlier in the fall, a little later in the winter. But as with the deciduous plants, if winters are very cold it is safer to wait till spring.

Read as rules, all this can seem restrictive and confusing—fine-print instructions to a new machine. Once in the garden, however, it is not like that. If one watches for a season or two, the rules are no longer rules, but respectful acknowledgments of what goes on.

Buying plants—delights and dangers

The garden center is a relatively new phenomenon and can confuse a gardener's sense of time. Not very long ago gardeners wanting to buy young plants had either to send away by mail or go to nurseries, the places where the plants were raised. Where I live there are still a few small retail nurseries where the growing is actually done on the premises and where ordinary home gardeners can go to buy perennial and annual flowers. Since several of the proprietors are getting on in years, I do not know how much longer the nurseries will remain.

I have to go to my local nurseries very early in the spring, before the trees are all leafed out. If I go any later, all the plants will be sold, and the owner will be back in the greenhouse seeding next year's plants. As it is, when I get there the cold frames are just opened and the field plants are newly dug. I spend an hour or two mulling over mossy pots, trying to guess from two or three purple shoots, a green whorl, maybe a leaf or two, which plants will be the strongest and how they will bloom, this year and in years to come. The growers, Joe, if it is one nursery, or Fleurette, if it is the other, come over from time to time and lean over my shoulder to make a recommendation or tell me about something new they are trying. We swap news of the previous season: what failed and what thrives in the garden and in our families. I leave with perhaps a dozen young plants, so small that they all fit in a single cardboard box. Often my hands are red with cold from standing so long in the damp spring air, but always my heart and imagination are warm with expectation.

Garden centers do not usually grow their plants. Instead they get deliveries from big wholesale nurseries somewhere else. Trucks pull in at least once a week throughout the growing season, unloading five-foot delphiniums, perfumed lilies, ancient oaks in ball and burlap. Everything is exquisite, ready grown and fully achieved. The containers in which the plants grow are so big, and there is so much potting soil around them, that it is possible, with care and the right manpower, to simply insert the plants, flowers and all, into the garden without ruffling a petal.

I am not sure how this is for the plants. I have tried it—planted roses in full bloom in June, asters in September, with mostly good luck and some bad (in postmortems I have discovered that the bad experiences are usually when the roots have failed to make their way out of the potting medium). But I know that for me it does not work so well. Garden centers are convenient and I would miss them; sometimes I find just the plant I am looking for, or one that surprises me; there is much to be learned in them. But often I leave filled with greed and a strange despair. In Goethe's *Faust,* Mephistopheles makes Faust his famous offer: Faust gets all knowledge, all power, all experience. On the devil's side, should

Faust ever be lured by a passing moment to say, "Stay! Thou art so fair," Faust's soul will be damned forever. I think the devil sometimes lurks in a garden center, still making the same deal. He wants me to believe that my garden should be frozen in some specious prime, denying the plant the opportunity to grow and wither, and the gardener the chance to watch it happen. When I hear him over my shoulder, I take a deep breath, remind myself that gardens perpetually die and become, then go home to do some weeding and see what might be coming on.

Propagating

Something is almost always coming on. Beyond reasons of beauty and tidiness, gardeners have to rearrange their gardens because plants continually multiply themselves. Many plants will try to populate the whole garden by lavishly reseeding. Gardeners who weed with a light hand will be delighted to find little foxgloves, feverfews, hollyhocks, columbines, and even tomatoes appearing all by themselves. At first they just pop out and surprise new gardeners with their bloom: ox-eyed daisies among the peony foliage, a lupine in the spinach row. Eventually one comes to recognize their early leaves, and on rainy days can take a trowel and move these friendly volunteers to the places where one would like them to grow.

Besides self-seeding, many plants increase by

making more of themselves. They form big clumps of roots that can be divided: phlox, for example, or mint, or rhubarb. Rhizomes (those gnarly stems that grow beneath the surface of the soil) spread sideways. Bearded iris and lily-of-the-valley multiply that way; left to themselves they could fill a bed. Bulbs (daffodils, for instance, and lilies) make new little bulbs around the old ones that eventually separate. Or a plant may layer itself, dropping a low-growing stem onto the soil, where it forms its own roots: one sees this in woody plants such as lavender, rosemary, or pinks.

This generosity of the plants sometimes tempts me to just let go and see what happens. I have seen abandoned gardens with wild hazes of purple asters and forests of phlox. But I know this unearthly beauty is just a stage toward wilderness. Gardens are about containment as well as fecundity. Harmony and balance, since Eden, have had to be supplied by the gardener.

ROOT DIVISION

Intervening in propagation is essential to gardening. Some garden plants degenerate if they are not divided. Big clumps of chrysanthemum go dead in the middle. Phlox in delicate hues revert to an ugly magenta. Others really do invade—even the evening primrose, so innocently shiny and yellow, takes on a sinister aspect when it covers the entire surface of the soil, strangling new shoots of less aggressive plants before they can properly emerge.

Making new plants from old is called husbandry, a very satisfying activity. This is how to create drifts and clumps without resorting to "three for twenty-five dollars" in the catalogues or succumbing to the temptations of the garden center. It is quite usual to end up with more plants than there is room for. These one can share with gardening friends, which is a most important aspect of gardening.

Once I asked about some tiny, indigo irises I saw blooming in a friend's garden early in the spring. He did not know what they were called, but told me how he had come upon them. On a hiking expedition in the Pyrenees mountains, he had stopped for a midday nap by the side of the stony path, his head among some spiky leaves. When he woke and opened his eyes, he found himself surrounded by lucid, blue flowers that had also opened while he slept, in a kind of azure image of awakening. Very carefully, so as not to damage the rest of the clump, he took a tiny root division and brought it home in his shoe.

Because I liked the story and the iris, he gave me a little root of my own. A few years later he called to tell me his irises had been killed by heaving frosts over the winter. How were mine? They had thrived, multiplied in fact, so that there were enough to restock his garden and still have plenty left for me. This is often how things go when gardeners share their plants.

In making root divisions of flowering plants, one follows the same timing as in simply transplanting them: right after flowering if they bloom early, as early as possible in spring if they flower late. Shallow-rooted plants are the easiest: chrysanthemum, evening primrose, bee balm, wild geranium. They are quick to dig up. The roots come apart very easily to make new clumps, one simply uses scissors or one's hands.

Plants with deeper, fibrous roots—like phlox, daylilies, Japanese anemones—need more digging. Once they are out, a quick thrust with a good, sharp spade, or sometimes the kitchen knife, will sever them. If the roots are really tangled, one might have to resort to pulling them apart with digging forks. It is surprising how much hacking most plants will withstand, as long as they are well watered and composted afterward. If a plant has grown tired at the middle (one sees this most clearly in early spring, when a circle of green shoots appears with an empty center), that middle section should be thrown away and only the lively outer parts replanted. The same is true of rhizomes, like the fat bearded-iris ones: if the rhizomes look shriveled and worn, abandon them and replant only the plump parts with healthy "eyes." Since this work necessarily means exposing roots to sky, it should always be done under a cloud or in the rain.

CUTTINGS

Making new plants from cuttings or layering is an experience no gardener should miss, if only to watch the miraculous phenomenon of one plant part becoming another. Scented geraniums are good plants with which to begin. They all "take" well, are easy-

going and quick to root. And there are so many varieties: plain and variegated, tiny pink blossoms and large-petaled white ones, scents of ginger, lemon, mint, and rose. There is bound to be one of which one would like to have more.

Choosing a moment when the parent plant is looking stocky and robust, one cuts a small side branch on the diagonal with a clean, sharp knife. From this one removes most of the leaves, leaving perhaps two. The nearly bare little stem is then set in some sand in a pot; below the sand is a little screened compost, and a pebble covers the drainage hole.

I keep my cuttings on the kitchen windowsill, where I can watch them while I am washing up and make sure they are always damp. In about three weeks the stem will have become a root and a new plant will be born, ready to be planted out. The poet Roethke saw the decisive moment:

> One nub of growth
> Nudges a sand-crumb loose,
> Pokes through a musty sheath
> Its pale tendrilous horn.

After this a gardener might be inspired to move on to other, more difficult plants. Many shrubs propagate quite easily from stem cuttings, and one feels especially proprietary toward a bush that was once a three-inch twig. It is possible, with patience, to make cuttings of stems or leaves or roots of almost any plant, even roses!

LAYERING

Layerings are done outside where the parent plant is growing. I make rosemary layerings every year; sometimes they make themselves. When I notice a low branch, I take off some of the leaves, leaving just a few at the end of the branch; then, with a small pebble, I weight the stem till it touches the earth and I cover it lightly with soil. The green tip remains above the ground and the other end of the branch is still attached to the mother plant. In a few weeks, the branch beneath the soil will have grown its own roots.

I tug it lightly to make sure it is anchored. When it is, I can cut the branch that connects it to its mother plant and it will stand alone. In autumn I will move it.

BULBS

I have left bulb-planting to the last, although planting spring bulbs in autumn was the first gardening I ever did, aged around four, and this is probably true for many gardeners. Planting bulbs is not difficult, even for hands that are small and still fumbling. It can be a thrill simply to hold in one's hands those carefully wrapped packages—described in my bulb book as "self-contained bits of suspended plant life"—that will open in time to come.

Tulip bulbs are sleek and plump, daffodils gnarled and crinkly, as are hyacinths, whose brownness is tinged faintly mauve. Curled up inside each one is the flower already formed, waiting to be born. Once I saw a photograph of a hyacinth flower still inside its bulb, and I remembered it when my infant daughter was a few weeks old and still slightly hunched over, as she had been in the womb. I had taken one of her hands in each of mine and spread them wide apart, opening her little chest for the first time. To my amazement, peals of delighted laughter came pouring out, as though they were blossoms of that hyacinth, curled inside and waiting for release.

"Suspended bits of plant life" is the broadest definition of a bulb. That term includes the "true bulbs," like tulips, daffodils, and lilies, which are underground stems with buds at the center. Crocuses and gladioli are examples of corms, similar to true bulbs except that the bud forms on top (one can see it), and the corm dies away each year, a new one forming above the old. Dahlias and anemones are something else again. They are tubers, thickened roots from which new buds—the eyes—appear each year.

The quality shared by all bulblike plants is their self-containment: they can feed upon themselves. All evolved in harsh climates, as a device for keeping alive through long periods without water or nourishment. Thus tulips originated in Turkey, and daffodils were known in ancient Egypt; fritillaries have been found close to the Himalayas. This capacity is also what makes them such a boon to gardeners; they can travel around the world without damage. (American gardeners often order bulbs from Holland.) They can be safely stored in cupboards and garden sheds. After planting at the proper time, gardeners can forget all about their bulbs and they themselves will remember to appear.

Snowdrops, aconites, crocuses, narcissi, tulips, hyacinths, fritillaries (checked snake's head lilies, strange towering purple *F. persica*, and majestic crown imperials) and most lilies are planted in autumn. In gardens with hard frosts, tender spring bulbs like anemones, ranunculus, and freesias must be planted early in spring; they will still manage to flower later the same season. The last to be planted are the tropical summer bulbs: dahlias, gladioli, fragrant tuberoses, which have to wait till there is no frost at all.

The hardy bulbs will stay in the ground, many of them naturalizing and spreading. This is why one never cuts the leaves off bulbs that have flowered if one wants them to come back the following year. It is through their leaves that the plants receive the nourishment they will store for the future. Anemones, even where it is cold, sometimes will work their way down and surprise us by coming back another year. But usually, if one wants to save tender bulbs, one must dig them up, "cure" them in the sun for a few hours so they do not become moldy, and store them away in a cool, dry place over winter.

Hardy spring bulbs should be planted late enough in autumn that warm spells will not lure them into premature sprouting, but early enough to give them time to put down roots. The holes should usually be dug three or four times as deep as the bulb is tall. A little bone meal sprinkled at the bottom of the hole will help the flowers, especially if the soil is poor. Most bulbs, being delicate, look loveliest planted in little clusters, which usually become big clusters over the years. Rather than making tiny holes for each bulb, I dig trenches with my spade, put in some old manure and bone meal (if I have any), and lay down a clump all at once. This lets me see the whole configuration. After making trenches in the lawn, I carefully replace the turf; this will not stop the bulbs.

Planting spring bulbs is exercise for the imagination. Gardeners push wheelbarrows filled with bags of bulbs, trowels, spades, and bone meal over the dead leaves and black flowers of autumn, looking for good spots to plant. Skeletons of sunflowers hang their heavy seed heads to feed departing birds wheeling overhead. As they bury those gnarled onion shapes in the earth, gardeners gaze across half the year to green leaves, white stars, and golden trumpets.

Chapter 6 Weeding

Sometimes, there are people who go almost mad when they see
dandelions on their lawn. In that case they should take a spade and
dig them out. But then they should realize that there would not be
a lawn if dandelions could not grow.

Ehrenfried Pfeiffer, *Weeds and What They Tell*

You should be grateful for the weeds you have in your mind,
because eventually they will enrich your practice. If you have some
experience of how the weeds in your mind change into mental
nourishment, your practice will make remarkable progress.

Shunryu Suzuki, *Zen Mind, Beginner's Mind*

*T*he first gardens I knew were so carefully tended I
rarely saw a weed. I thought there was a rule against them. It was
a relief to grow up and discover that there are no rules in gardening, only laws of nature. One such law dictates that there is only so
much sunlight, water, and good soil to go around. So to the
degree that uninvited plants rob the chosen garden plants, one
could say "too many weeds." But especially where the soil is rich
and there is plenty of sun and rain, cultivated plants can coexist
with *some* uncultivated ones quite happily. Then the question of
how finely weeded the garden must be becomes one of the gardener's vision.

In the early days of gardening, a retreat from wilderness, the whole point of gardening was to grow only what the gardener intended. Many gardeners today still feel that way, and will not be at peace in their gardens until every last chickweed is plucked out. Other gardeners see their gardens as an interplay between what they intend and what nature interjects; such gardens tolerate, even welcome, some visitors from the weed world.

In the wide spectrum of weededness, more and more I have come to admire the particular radiance of gardens that are meticulously cultivated. I do not mean the mechanically clipped ones of my childhood; there the mood was too negative, too antiweed. The gardens I mean are those where one sees that each individual plant is cared for and loved, the soil raked carefully about the crowns, enough air and light flowing around each one to let it reveal its own singular form. I know a garden where the plants being cherished in this way are in fact the ones usually called "weeds" in other gardens (pokeweed, chicory, mullein, here carefully raised for butterflies and birds). It too is exquisite.

Small gardens, hand-worked by diligent, loving gardeners, have a luminous quality, in which even the humblest plants become specimens and speak. When I see this in a neighbor's garden, over a low village fence, on rare occasions in part of my own, I find myself thinking, "*This* is the way a garden should be."

My garden is not usually like that, and I am not sure that it ever can be for very long. Perhaps it is too big. Over the years its gentle sunny slope and the desires of my family called out for one flower border and then another and another, a vegetable garden, herbs, a bed for raspberries, currants, and gooseberries, a kind of lawn in the middle for running games, another hidden one off to one side, apple, pear, cherry, and peach trees, and a little rock garden. It all seems essential to us, but does not reconcile well with my typical late-twentieth-century life of working to pay bills, raising children, more or less keeping house. Often the whole garden seems on the verge of being swallowed by a tidal wave of burdock, grasses, spurge. But because I never do give up, but keep on steadily and happily weeding along as best I can, it never actually drowns. So I do not think it really is too big. Rather the weeds that remain are part of the garden.

I have found there is another kind of beauty, and some mystery, in the garden that gets away, goes a little wild, allows entry to the unexpected. In the neglected corners and fringes of my garden jimson weed, thistles, and burdock lurk, but so do sea lavender, rose mallow, blue chicory, Queen Anne's lace. With every rare discovery that surprises me as I carry the washing to the line I think, "*This* is the way a garden ought to be."

Liberty Bailey, whose knowledge of cultivated plants filled three volumes of his great *Encyclopedia Hortus,* wrote (not in the encyclopedia):

> The man who worries night and morning about the dandelions in the lawn will find great relief in loving the dandelions. Each blossom is worth more than a gold coin, as it shines in the exuberant sunlight of the growing spring, and attracts the insects to its bosom. Little children like the dandelions: why may not we? Love the things nearest at hand, and love intensely.

By choice or by default, all gardens lean a bit more toward one side, a bit more toward the other. No garden stays the same. The most manicured garden will have its wild moment, if its gardener looks the other way for a week in summer. A garden that is usually tangled and overgrown can take on crystalline clarity after a day or two of concentrated weeding. My garden is like a beach at which the tide goes in and out. Sometimes the tide of weeds is out, and the plants stand clear and lovely. Sometimes the tide is in, bringing its wrack of pigweed, nettle, mallows, and wild roses. This is lovely in another way.

Weeding as pastime

Whatever one's goal of weededness, the real secret of weeding is to enjoy it. Weeding has a bad name. One learns to avoid it, often before one even finds out how to do it.

"I'm just going out to weed the flower bed."

"Oh, poor you."

But no one would feel it necessary to sympathize if the person headed out the door were dressed in running shoes or carrying bird-watching binoculars, though these activities, too, call for intense exercise and patient observation. Fooled by weeding's reputation, it was some years before I noticed how much I liked it.

One year, my brother took up surf casting on the winter beach. Once in a while he caught a fish, which was nice, but I mostly remember his explaining that with a rod in his hand he could stand gazing at the gulls and breaking waves for hours at a time. Without the rod this was more awkward. In some ways this is how I feel about my hoe and the hours in the garden it entitles me to spend. Weeding needs attention, but not the intently focused attention of planting or pruning. The slow, contemplative weeding done by hand around tiny seedlings allows a gardener to smell sap and pollen, hear bird songs, notice the shadows of clouds. Thoughts settle down the spine and tension leaves through the fingertips, earthing itself in the soil.

The other kind of weeding, when the weeds have already sent down tough grasping roots and are about to engulf the plants, is different, but can be satisfying in another way. Fast, heavy, and hot, it needs both arms, a wheelbarrow, and a hoe. Quite often (most often when life confronts me with a frustrating situation I can do nothing about), it is what I most feel like doing. When I am finished, I feel tired but restored. The garden, which had almost slipped out of focus, regains its fine edges and possibilities. The work is rough and wild, but the results are radiant and delicate.

I do not want to be unduly romantic; no one can love weeding if the weeds always get ahead. To keep at it, as one must, it is necessary to see that one's efforts have effects. For this one needs strategies. There is no single panacea; different parts of the garden call for different approaches, as do different sorts of weeds. But in looking more closely at what is at work in each situation, much frustration can be avoided, and enjoyment, even interest, increased.

Weeding annuals and vegetables

The simplest, though not always the lightest, weeding is in the vegetable garden, or anywhere all the plants are annuals. This is because one can begin with a kind of blank slate. In chapter 2 it was mentioned that one should wait at least two weeks to plant a bed after digging it over or forking it through in spring. This is to let the soil settle. But that pause is also an essential weeding strategy. Preparing the soil wakes the weed seeds that have wintered over. In two or three weeks they will show their first leaves. A quick surface hoeing then will be all that is needed to be rid of them. Then one can plant the seeds knowing they have gained a head start.

How long the garden plants keep this advantage depends on how soon they germinate and how fast they grow. Quick spring greens will seldom be overtaken, especially if they have been sown thickly in a bed. Lettuce planted this way will soon need thinning, but hardly ever any weeding. But among slow, upright plants, leeks, for instance, or parsnips, there will be room and time for a new generation of weeds to grow in the spaces between. When this begins to happen, it is time to find a comfortable spot to sit beside the bed and reach in to pull them out. Fingers are best for this kind of weeding. No tool is as precise, and one can feel with them to make sure one has hold of the whole root and to avoid encroaching on another plant.

Where spaces between plants are wider, between bean rows for instance, or among young tomato plants, scratching with a sharp hoe will prevent new weeds from starting or put an end to any that may be rushing ahead. This kind of light stirring, never more than an inch or two deep, not only weeds the bed but keeps the soil permeable to moisture and air. It is better not to do this too often, especially if the soil is looking powdery, just enough to keep ahead and prevent a crust from forming. One might form the habit of carrying a hoe, like a staff, on garden strolls, striking here and there as needed, often not at all. About once a month, I bring a wheelbarrow and shovel and combine this light cultivation with a thin mulching of compost or leaf mold.

Weeding perennial beds

Weeding in an established perennial bed is a more subtle and delicate matter than cultivating vegetables. It is also more interesting. Because the bed is pervaded by the roots—some straight and hoary, some fine and spreading—of its permanent plants, it is impossible to work with the broad strokes one might use to prepare a carrot planting. Especially in early spring, when not all the plants are up, one needs to remember where every peony or bellflower is growing and to work very carefully until the last marshmallow or tiger lily breaks the surface.

It is true that one can mark the plants each autumn, and this is a great help when it comes to spring weeding. But in my garden squirrels and children and frost-heavings displace many of my little wooden tags: then I count on memory, and where memory fails, on caution. Besides preserving the returning "permanent" plants, there are also infants to protect. Perennial beds are always also nursery beds, birthplace of new plants from self-sown seed or from rhizomes spreading underground. At least half of the plants in my flower bed were born there. If I had weeded too strenuously they would not exist.

For these reasons I weed the perennials in spring only very slowly, pulling out one weed at a time, using only my hands and never pulling out anything till I am quite sure what it is. Weeding a perennial bed is the best schooling for a gardener's eye. This is where one learns to tell the seed leaves of a delphinium from those of a buttercup, a Michaelmas daisy from a spurge. A gardener might nurture a plant or clump of plants for ten summer weeks only to discover when the flower buds open at last that he or she has cultivated fleabane and weeded out the Japanese anemones. Should this happen, that gardener should take comfort in the thought that such mistakes are entirely honorable and of an ancient tradition. There is no other way to learn the changing forms of the plants from seed leaves to blossom except by watching them grow.

Around the time of the summer solstice, the situation changes. All the plants are now above ground and one need not be quite so watchful. In fact, one really can't be. Unless the bed is very small or one is a full-time gardener, the weeds grow so fast that it is impossible to keep up with them one at a time. In July and August, I resort to tools.

The hoes and tined cultivators designed for vegetable gardens are too big and clumsy for working in between perennials. What is needed are tools that can reach into tight corners, cut precisely, aerate the soil's surface, but not dig so deep down that they will damage friendly roots or cause the soil to clod and cake. Such tools do exist, but sometimes one has to look for them. Using a small three-pronged cultivator is a nice refinement. If the soil is already clear of visible weeds, it will prevent new annual weeds from starting and keep the soil lively, and it can also be used to work in top dressings of compost. But the essential tool, once weeds are up, is a knife-sharp hoe, no more than four inches wide.

Both the cultivator and hoes can be found in short-handled

models for working on one's knees, or with long
handles, for working standing up. My
indispensable short-handled hoe is the
Japanese one I ordered from Smith &
Hawken ten years ago, as sharp now as
when I bought it. It is still available for
about ten dollars. My best long-handled model is a swan-neck hoe, a sharp
blade on a six-foot handle, which can
be ordered from Gardener's Supply
Company. I like to use the short-handled
tools best, because I prefer, when I can, to
work close to the ground, where I can still
keep an eye on new chance seedlings. Flat

stones or sections of tree trunk set here and there inside the bed
make good crouching places to work from without compacting
the soil. But as summer deepens and it gets more and more difficult to move around without stepping on a shoot or breaking a
branch, I use the long-handled hoe that lets me reach almost anywhere from outside the bed.

Around the end of September, when the air cools and clears,
there is a moment of grace when suddenly the garden plants reju-
venate and the weeds slow down. Then it becomes possible to
pull out weeds one at a time again. Autumn has perfect weeding
weather, mild sunshine, blue mists in which to contemplate the
turning year, and it is good gardening practice to clean the beds of
weeds and any diseased plant matter before winter to prevent any
festering. I usually find some summer seedlings that have survived
my indiscriminate August hoeing, often foxgloves, maybe holly-

hocks. I mark and sometimes move them and give them a little compost to encourage them to stay through the winter.

Annual weeds and perennial weeds

There are weeds and weeds. Annual weeds—like amaranth, chickweed, smartweed, and pigweed—do not live long, but they reproduce themselves so quickly that they can seem immortal. For this reason it is much better if one can catch the annuals before they go to seed. Flowers are a good warning, but pigweed blossoms and many others are hard to spot, so it is best to get them young.

Perennial weeds are more difficult to manage. They do not always show up during the first seasons of the garden. Like trees in a forest, weeds in the garden come and go in succession, and perennial weeds are usually a later stage. Perhaps it takes a little while for the ground to realize that the gardener is serious about keeping it open. Once it catches on, the ground seems to get just as serious about covering itself up. Often it will choose a grass to do the job, usually couchgrass, with rhizomes that cling and clutch like the pincers of crabs.

Realizing that some part of the garden is being invaded by roots rapidly spreading underground, a gardener might be inclined to panic. The seemingly obvious line of attack, finding the roots and pulling them out hand over hand, is usually futile. No matter how carefully one pulls, some segments of root break off and remain in the soil. These regenerate very quickly and soon the tangled web is back. Even digging over the whole bed and forking it through rarely works because some last strands always remain deep in the subsoil. If I am going to double dig anyway, of course I pull out every thread I can see, but I will no longer dig up a whole bed just to get at the weeds. It is too infuriating when they resurrect the following spring.

Two strategies work. One is for the more manageable cases, the other for when things seem truly to have got out of hand. The first technique is to simply exhaust the plants. No plant can survive indefinitely without leaves, so if one keeps hoeing off the tops the plant will, eventually, lose its will to live. This is the kind of weeding that one does for exercise, and I find enough can be achieved by means of fast, intense flurries among the couchgrass or leafy spurge about once a week in summer.

It can happen, under certain conditions, that the grasses start to grow so thick and fast that they make a mockery of anything one tries to plant. Luckily, this usually only happens in one or two beds at a time, seldom throughout an entire garden. There is a remedy, but it is not a quick one. It is a kind of truce. The garden wants to be covered, so one covers it. What is needed is a cover crop with vigorous roots that will restore the broken connections in the soil and, at the same time, smother the weeds.

I have used a succession of white clover and winter rye, but a Rodale published book, *Start with the Soil* by Grace Gershuny, suggests two sowings of buckwheat, followed by rye, as the most effective remedy specifically for couchgrass. The buckwheat is sown first in early spring, cut down and turned in when it starts to flower, then sown again, and turned in at the end of summer just as it starts to flower again. Then rye is planted in fall, covers the ground thickly all winter, and is cut down and turned in again in early spring. (See Readings and Resources for sources of cover crop seeds and advice on planting.)

This is a long process, but it makes a certain sense. If one finds oneself locked in combat with the garden, it is usually time to back off, rather than to press on regardless. A light sprinkling of couchgrass is a warning to pay more attention to the soil: add compost, plant deep-rooted crops or legumes if one has been growing shallow or hungry ones, then seed clover in the fall and turn it in before it flowers in the spring. But a serious couchgrass invasion says, "Enough! This soil needs rest!" Until the gardener hears this, the couchgrass will keep saying it and will not go away.

Time, weather, and weeding

At high noon on a bright day, weeds cling like barnacles to the dry earth. No one could love weeding in that heat and dust. The garden does not like it either; soil should not be opened in the midday sun. And plants already distressed by heat want no further disturbance. The best time for weeding is when the garden is still moist from a good rain or heavy morning dew, the soil damp but not sodden. (If the soil is so wet that it will not shake off the roots, one needs to wait till it will.) Then weeds come out readily at a tug, roots and all. The work goes fast, the plants look grateful, and the moist greenness refreshes the gardener's spirits.

When there is a real drought, I leave all but the most vigorous of my weeds alone. This is controversial. Some gardeners say it is important to weed in a drought because the weeds will rob the plants of scarce water. But in gardening one must act on what one sees where one is, and in my garden the soil stays moister and more lively if shaded by leaves and penetrated by roots, whether the leaves and roots are those of my own chosen plants or those of weeds.

Disposing of weeds

Leafy annual weeds, like nettles and chickweed, make excellent compost ingredients. They are rich in nitrogen and minerals. But there is always the concern that in adding the seeds of annuals or the rhizomes and roots of perennial weeds to the pile, one will only end up propagating more weeds than ever when the compost comes to be spread.

I put all my weeds in the compost anyway. This is because the compost I make, as described in chapter 3, gets hot. Compost that heats up to 130 degrees will kill most weed seeds. Whether it will also kill couchgrass rhizomes is less clear. I try to keep an eye on my most dangerous seeds and roots, and layer the pile so that they are as close as possible to the center where the heat will be most intense. I assemble my compost heap in fall and usually can no longer recognize the weeds I have pulled out several months before, so I think—perhaps naively—that if the plant is so decomposed as to have lost its form, it is unlikely to have the force to regenerate.

I know that *all* the seeds are not killed, and certainly not all the rhizomes, because of the lamb's-quarters and grasses that always sprout on the surface of my compost heap in springtime. But I can live with this, upending the top layer with my pitchfork, turning the pile once or twice before I spread it on the garden.

Where I grew up, in damp England, gardeners routinely burned their brush and weeds in garden bonfires. A lot of good organic matter was lost this way; some gardeners even burned their autumn leaves. But if one's weed problems are getting particularly bad, burning the seed heads and rhizomes is a most effective purge.

Gardeners who have no time or interest in making hot compost, and who are forbidden bonfires by local ordinance, can set up extremely long-term weed composts and leave them to crumble into the indefinite future. Or, if they live in forward-looking communities, they might look into their local municipal composting arrangements. Most of these compost under cover and at such high temperatures (to kill pathogens) that they will knock out any weed seeds. But the manager of my local compost plant suspects that couchgrass rhizomes can survive even these and would rather people did not bring them in.

Reading weeds

The final and most important weeding strategy is curiosity, and no one can weed for very long without becoming curious. No two gardens have quite the same weeds, and no one garden has the same weeds for very long. The questions seem to grow out of

the ground. What are those with the purple flowers and hairy leaves? Why these last year and not this? Why those this year and not last? Which bird-sown or wind-blown seeds colonize? Which remain solitary hermits and never come again? This summer a jimson weed has appeared and is towering beside the pear tree. It is a poisonous plant, so I cannot let it flower and set seed, but I cannot bring myself to cut it down till I see how high it will grow. Already it is eight feet tall, with leaves the size of tables.

The names of the weeds are stories in themselves: lamb's-quarters, fleabane, goosegrass, cheat. I love to learn them, but it is not so easy, especially if one has not grown up in the same place as one now gardens. The same weeds can look very different in different terrains; or sometimes they look the same but go by a different name. Then there will always be new ones, never seen before. Wildflower guides are helpful up to a point, but not very useful when one is looking at docks and pigweeds and other visitors not notable for conspicuous flowers. The best weed guide I know, with good black-and-white drawings, is the United States Department of Agriculture's *Common Weeds of the United States*. (Published in 1970, it has been kept in print not by the government, but by the invaluable Dover Press.) And if one is fortunate enough to have a natural history society in one's neighborhood, one might learn not only a name, but at least part of a story.

Weeds always do have a story. Knowing it sheds light on both the weed and the garden. A stray breeze may blow seeds on thistle-down parachutes into the garden, but whether a few thistles sprout as brief visitors, or whether they stay and take over whole beds, depends on the condition of the garden. Smartweed likes wet, acid soil, so it thrives in the low, stagnant spots on my lawn. I can pull it out all I like, but it will never go away till I tend to those spots, turn them over, grade them, and cultivate the soil-texture till it becomes loose, friable, and able to drain. But not all weeds tell bad news. If lamb's-quarters and purslane thrive among my vegetables, it is because they love the rich, healthy soil there.

Weeds and What They Tell, by Ehrenfried Pfeiffer, is a short book that, as its title suggests, classifies the world of weeds according to their stories. Written forty years ago but kept continuously in print, first by Rodale and then by the Bio-Dynamic Press, it is a book that introduced me to my own garden. Weed visitations, though still perplexing, no longer seemed random. I began to see that some came because I invited them, others because of a more ancient history, still others actually to help.

The first class of weeds that Pfeiffer defines is that of the weeds that flourish (as nothing else will) where soils are in difficulty. They "tell us by their mere presence what is wrong." Docks, ox-eyed daisies, my smartweed, and horsetail all indicate an acid soil. Such a soil on a farm or in a garden might not be inherently acidic, but may have been soured by overcultivation and not enough humus, or perhaps it has become acidic through poor drainage: it gets so wet that air cannot penetrate it. Then there are the weeds that thrive on a hard, crusted surface. Perhaps one did not begin with such a surface, but it might be creeping in through working the soil when it is too wet, or growing too many successions of the same kinds of plants in the same place. "Chamomile," one of the benign weeds, "warns you in a friendly way to change your rotation," writes Pfeiffer. "If you do not change, you will invite the wild mustard gangsters."

Another weed category is that of the weeds that come because they love cultivated ground and composted soil. Purslane, plantain, spurge, all congregate "wherever man walks." Pfeiffer, himself a plant breeder and student of plant metamorphoses, takes a keen interest in these plants, points out their relationship to cultivated plants of the same families (shepherd's purse, for instance, being cousin to the cabbage), and looks prophetically into the future. For example, he points to the weeds in the goosefoot (*Chenopodiaceae*) family, which he feels "were destined to play another role than that as an obnoxious weed."

They follow closely man's steps showing their inclination to be domesticated. Probably future plant breeders may develop new cultivated varieties out of this family long after our present cultivated plants have degenerated, for it is their extreme vitality and perseverance to grow that makes the Goosefoot family so interesting.

These days *Chenopodium quinoa,* once a grain that grew only in the high Andes, is cultivated in Oregon, and I can buy it in my local health-food shop. It is sweet and nutlike, one of the most nourishing of cereals. Cultivated orach is a tasty new salad ingredient, grown by market gardeners. Both are goosefoots and close relatives of the lamb's-quarters (which, incidentally, are delicious picked young and steamed with garlic) that grow all over my vegetable beds. I have to wonder what other "weeds" of today have the potential to become the cabbage and potatoes of tomorrow.

Another category of "weed," not necessarily intrusive, is comprised of those plants whose nature it is to thrive at the edges between woods and hedgerows and cleared land. Pfeiffer describes these as "more or less extensions of nature into the realm of man." Among them are some wild members of the rose family and "the pleasant weeds of the Pink and the useful Legume families." Where broom, wild alfalfa, and clover—all legumes—grow, a spontaneous restoration of a depleted soil can be seen in progress.

Finally Pfeiffer draws some fascinating portraits of the "dynamic" weed plants that in their pure, wild state carry a particular vitality that cultivated plants lack and that can be seen to have a "medicinal" effect on what grows around them. Nettles, for instance, produce a neutral humus around their roots and stimulate the flavor and growth of nearby crops. Dandelion, with its long taproot, draws to the surface of the soil essential minerals, especially calcium, that would otherwise be unavailable to plants. "We could almost say that what the earthworm as an animal does to the soil, the dandelion as a plant does also." Pfeiffer notes from his own experience (raising, for example, nettles for compost in Egypt) that, although the dynamic weeds may be difficult to eradicate, they can also be hard to introduce. They seem to grow only where the situation requires them, and to leave only when it is mended.

The book makes no pretense at being complete, though it is dense with anecdote and allusion. It belongs to a rare and precious class of book: short and light, but written with the experience of a life of monumental achievement. Pfeiffer was a biochemist, agronomist, and farmer, and as a young man in Switzerland in the 1920s he worked closely with Rudolf Steiner to pioneer biodynamic agriculture. He devoted his life (the latter part spent in America) to developing quality tests, plant-breeding, perfecting composting methods, farming, researching, consulting, and lecturing to promote biodynamic methods, a daunting task in a world that was deeply into chemical agriculture and far from ready for an approach to agriculture based on a sensitive apprehension of nature.

His book leaves much open-ended. All kinds of questions come to mind: what about this plant, or that? to what category does it belong? what if it seems to fit into several at once? what is the essential *character* of each plant? But the raising of these questions was clearly the author's intention and central to his own methods. He makes it impossible to contemplate weeds without wonder. Each detail—the tiny white stars that flower on a chick-weed, the bitter taste of wormwood—is significant. "Weeds want to tell a story. . . . If we could only listen to it, we could apprehend the finer forces through which Nature helps and heals and balances and, sometimes, also has fun with us."

> When I looked under the hedge—
> the little grass called shepherd's purse
> was flowering.
>
> Basho

Chapter 7 *Pruning*

If a person cannot love a plant after he has pruned it, then he has
either done a poor job or is devoid of emotion.

Liberty Hyde Bailey, *The Pruning Book*

A friend of mine, who had been strictly, perhaps too
strictly, brought up and sent to very regimented schools, moved
into a little house with a garden full of flowering shrubs and
refused to prune any of them. He said that human beings had
interfered with nature too much. Now that he had a quarter acre
of his own he wanted to leave it in peace.

For the first few years the garden took on a romantic dishevel-
ment. But as time passed, it grew dark and melancholy. The
bushes overshadowed themselves, their trunks bare at the bottom,
and they flowered less and less—although their top growth got so
thick my friend could no longer see out of his windows. Then he
married a woman who loved both him and plants. She convinced
him that not all restriction is repressive, that cutting back, done
right, brings vigor, flower, and fruit. Their garden now is full of
blossoms, light, and new green shoots.

Planting, transplanting, and weeding is when gardeners meet
their plants. In pruning the relationship gets closer. To prune a
plant one must join in with its growing. There is nothing quite
like it. The dictionary says that pruning means removing superflu-

ous growth. That is certainly part of the story, but not the end of it. In plants, as in life, it is often not till the superfluous is removed that the essential can be revealed.

Liberty Bailey makes a useful distinction between pruning and shearing. In his vocabulary, shearing means forcing a plant into a given shape or keeping it to a particular size; pruning is for vigor and to cause a plant to be more "floriferous and fruitful." The experience of each is quite different. When I shear I feel I am bending a plant to my own ends, and when I prune I pay attention to what the plant is doing and take direction from that.

How pruning works: balance and buds

Any plant produces many more buds than it could possibly turn into leaves, branches, or fruit. In nature a plant will be pruned by storms or by grazing or, most often, by overshadowing from its own branches or those of other plants. In perfect conditions—the optimal harmony of soil, climate, and plant—a plant will grow all by itself into perfect health and beauty. Such conditions do not often occur, so the gardener compensates and helps the plant by pruning selectively.

Sawing dead wood out of an oak tree is pruning; so is shaping and thinning an apple tree so as to have fruit to eat. Snipping off the lilac flowers when they turn brown to make sure there will be more flowers next year is pruning, so is cutting entire trunks to the ground when the whole lilac bush needs renewing. When I pinch off the top bud on a cosmos, so as to have a fat plant with many blossoms instead of a tall thin one with few, that is pruning, and so is taking the side shoots off a tomato plant to get more tomatoes.

Pruning is difficult to read about: on paper it can sound bewildering. Only in the garden does it really make sense. Like riding a bicycle, it is best learned by getting on with it. So as soon as possible a gardener should find good, sharp tools and go out and make a beginning. Some preparation is of course necessary, but I find that the most useful kind is not so much diagrams showing where to cut (which do not always seem to correspond with the plant one is actually facing) as a review of some basic growth processes in plants. The processes with which a pruner is concerned have to do with balance and with the nature of buds.

Plants always strive to maintain a balance between what is below the earth (roots) and what is above it (stems, branches, leaves, and flowers). Therefore when one wants to cut through roots to transplant an iris, say, or a rose, one must first reduce what is growing above the ground—snipping the iris leaves or shortening the rose stems—so that the diminished roots will not be overwhelmed. By the same principle of balance, if one cuts back leaves and branches in a plant where the roots are intact, the roots will be stimulated to send up new growth to restore what has been lost. This is how pruning works.

Anyone who has seen a rosebush that has been chewed by a rabbit will notice how quickly that plant will send out lush new growth to replace what has been lost. A pruning gardener does the same as the rabbit, but tries to direct that growth in particular directions. Gardeners do this by working with buds.

Just as a plant will make many more seeds than could actually find room to germinate, in order to compensate for those that will be damaged, eaten, or go astray, it also, and for the same reason, makes more buds than it would be able to carry if they all opened. In planting one spaces seeds to make sure they have enough light and space to unfold into plants. In pruning one cultivates buds, searching out those that are in the best places and giving them encouragement and light.

In most plants, growth is focused at the tips of the branches, the growing points. If the terminal (outermost) bud is removed, the buds beneath it are awakened and they become the new growing points. In shrubs and trees there is a terminal bud at the tip of every branch. Looking at a lilac twig in early spring one can see that it is the bud at the tip that looks fattest and ready to go. The ones just below are a little leaner, but clearly on the way to becoming. Farther down there will be flat little buds so small that they might perhaps not be buds at all. These are dormant and will only fatten into growth if they turn out to be needed. The same is true of the invisible buds, the mere possibility of buds, that are hidden under the skin of the branch. They too will come into being only if they are needed. As long as the terminal bud stays intact, the dormant buds sleep on.

To see how buds work, one might begin where the results of pruning will be seen very quickly. Snipping off the first flower bud of a cornflower or another simple annual flower in spring will cause new side branches to sprout in a few days, each with its own flower buds. Soon the whole plant will look sturdier, more solidly anchored in the ground than its spindly, unpruned neighbors. (For a counterexample, consider the giant sunflower, where one usually wants a single enormous flower on one tall stalk and for which one must leave the terminal bud untouched.) If one cuts the faded flower spike down to the ground after a delphinium has bloomed, in a week or so the root will send out a whole new shoot that will flower later in the summer.

Pruning shrubs and roses

Having gained confidence in renewal by removal, a gardener might move on to pruning woody plants, those that do not die back to the ground each year—shrubs, vines, and trees. While the principle remains the same, this gets more complicated than pruning herbaceous plants because one needs to know something about the particular growing habits of each one. When I was little, I used to watch my mother stride into the garden, and, clipper in hand, attack a grapevine or a mock orange. I thought she knew some single thing that I too would know when I grew up. It was dismaying to discover, in taking care of my own garden, that what my mother knew was not one thing, but many.

Having gardened now for as long as my mother had then, I too know many single things, for instance that in my garden apple trees need pruning in February, roses in April, the viburnum sometime in May, the yews in June. I know this kind of thing about each of the thirty or forty kinds of shrubs and trees in my garden, but I cannot imagine that I could have learned it all at once. Luckily one seldom needs to. Most bushes and trees do not need pruning every year, many hardly ever, and quite a lot never. So it is possible, and much better, to learn to prune one plant at a time.

When one prunes a flowering shrub or a fruiting tree depends on when and where it forms its buds. Some shrubs, roses for instance, only make flower buds on new green shoots that have grown the same year as the flowers will open. Others, mostly the kinds that flower early in the season, like quince, witch hazel, or forsythia, form their flower buds during the summer before (on "old wood"). Thus if I go out in early spring and cut back the old rose stems of my Queen Elizabeth rose to where I see a promising bud, vigorous new green stems will grow out of each cut, all of which will have time to make flower buds between April and June. If on the other hand I went out on the same day and cut back the old wood on the lilacs to healthy buds, I would get new green shoots that would make plenty of new leafy growth, but there would be no flowers at all because all the flower buds had formed last summer on the tips of the branches that I cut away.

Observant gardeners could, over the years, figure these things out for themselves. It helps to realize that in general shrubs that flower in early spring have formed their flower buds the previous year and should never be cut till after flowering. Shrubs that flower later in summer form their flower buds in spring and can be cut very early that same spring. Furthermore, it is an interesting exercise to see if, by peering really hard, one can tell a flower bud from a leaf bud. But it is safest to back up one's best guess by looking up each shrub in gardening books of the encyclopedic type (see Readings and Resources at the back of the book for some suggestions).

Lilac is a good example of a patient, undemanding shrub that can live for a hundred years or more but still needs a gardener's attention, at certain moments, to stay bushy and full of bloom. One way to help keep a lilac flowering each year is to cut off all the flowers one can reach as soon as they start changing color from lilac to rusty brown. This keeps the blossoms from becoming seed-bearing fruit. It is a pattern among many woody plants not to make flower buds for next year on the same places where they have formed fruit. This is why if one leaves the flowers to fade, there will be fewer flowers next year (although in the case of a really healthy lilac bush, fewer can still be plenty).

If, even though one has been conscientious about deadheading its flowers every year, the lilac bush is still forming fewer and fewer flowers, and if it seems to be concentrating all its leaves at the top, leaving bare, leggy trunks below, it means that it is time to renew the bush. This is something one only needs to do every ten or fifteen years. But when the time comes, one knows: the bush is not what it was.

To renew a lilac bush, one waits till late in the winter, then takes a good saw and cuts each trunk down to a foot off the ground. The stumps look bleak and bare, but when spring comes the ancient root will have received the message to send out new green shoots, the trunks of the future. Gardeners should note that doing this kind of serious pruning means there will be no flowers for two years. This is one reason why many gardeners would rather skip it; for them, spring is not spring without the scent of lilac. But there are ways to soften the blow: one can stagger the pruning over two or three years, cutting down some of the trunks one year, some the next. Or one might plant more bushes, to make sure that at least one lilac will flower each May.

Most garden roses are at the opposite extreme from the easy-going lilac. They do need pruning every year. But sometimes not as much pruning as one might be led to fear. It all depends. Books on roses can be worrying because they usually stress that there are at least five main categories of rose types, each with several sub-categories—old shrub, modern hybrids, climbers, ramblers, and so on—and that each category has its own growth habit and there-fore requires its own pruning method. This is true, and I do not want to turn anyone away from rose books: specific information is invaluable and indeed is the essence of gardening. But a reader's confusion can be greatly diminished when a wise author steps back and gives the big picture, as in this lucid explanation from *Roses for English Gardens,* by Gertrude Jekyll and Edward Mawley:

> In the first place, it is the object of pruning to add vigour to a plant and at the same time to regulate its growth. It is difficult to understand at first, but nevertheless perfectly true, that the more severely a rose plant is pruned the stronger will be the

shoots which result from that apparently murderous treatment. There is also another general rule that arises out of the foregoing, and that is the weaker the plant the more closely it should be cut back, and the more vigorous it is the longer should the shoots be left.

With this guiding thought in mind it is actually possible to approach any rose even if, as sometimes happens, one is not quite sure what it is, and make some intelligent guesses as to what ought to be done. If it is a weak plant, consisting of one or two not very vigorous-looking shoots, the chances are it is a hybrid perpetual or hybrid tea, a grafted rose that bears big flowers, though few, on rather short, spindly plants. These are the kind that require the "murderous treatment," cut back every spring to three or four short pegs that then send out canes about three feet long with large flower buds at the end. If the rose in question is a big, healthy bush with a dozen sturdy canes five feet tall, or taller, it is a shrub rose, and usually needs very gentle pruning or none at all.

For any gardener afraid of pruning roses, there is no substitute for getting hold of a sharp and solid pair of hand pruners (the kind with blades that overlap are best for cutting close to buds) and simply beginning. Luckily, roses are not pruned all at once, but little by little, as the year progresses. This gives gardeners the chance to feel their way.

The first steps are the same regardless of what sort of rose it is: clearing out and thinning. When it seems that winter is over, but before anything besides onion grass and spring peepers have really come to life, it is time to wander over to the roses to see how they came through. Any shoots or side shoots that have died over the winter or that look unhealthy will need cutting out. This will give the rose the room to bud out freely as spring comes. It is not always easy to tell so early what is alive and what is dead. Sometimes it is obvious—one cane is black and hollow at the tip, another mottled and diseased, a few encouragingly green. When, as is often the case, the canes are an enigmatic grayish brown, one waits.

I like this looking and guessing, intuiting what is dead and what is alive. I am often wrong, so I always check, cutting off an inch or two to look inside. If the pith is dark brown the stem is dead, if white and milky it is alive. Sometimes it is just the tip that is brown, so I always cut little by little till I find live wood and stop there. But if the cane seems sickly or might get in the way of another, it is better to cut it all the way back, down to the union (the lumpy mass low on the main stem where the rose is grafted), or to the main stem if the cane in question is a side shoot.

Thinning is not just good for the rose, it is very good for the gardener. If one goes slowly and carefully, no serious damage will result, and with each cut one is conversing with the rose, hearing what it has to say about where it wants to go this year. The dialogue reopens, usually a few weeks later, when the rose presents its first strong buds. Again the first step is a pause and a long look. Which of these buds is the fattest and firmest? Which is likely to send out the most vigorous green cane to make a strong framework for the plant? If the rose is healthy there will be several contenders. Then one considers the direction in which they are pointing and decides which of those would most help the rose.

Roses originated in hot, dry places. They love sunlight and dry air, and suffer from damp and stagnation, the cause of fungus diseases. Therefore the main object in pruning roses is to open the plants up to sun and air and prevent them from shading and crowding themselves. This means looking for buds that point outward away from the center of the plant and making sure that branches do not cross or overshadow each other too closely.

This principle of an open center is the same in hybrid teas, where one will be cutting the two or three main canes down to healthy buds a few inches from the union, and in the shrub roses, where one basically lets the tall canes stand and lightly prunes the side shoots to make sure they have room to grow and do not cross. The cuts are carefully made about an inch above a bud and angled away from it (this is so that water drips away from the bud rather than onto it). If the rose is quite old, and there are one or two old canes that no longer seem up to much, one might cut them down to the ground to allow new ones to form and replace them.

As spring progresses, gardeners continue to visit their roses, watching to see what the buds will actually do, which is not always quite what they intended. Often the pruning continues. Sometimes I see I have made a poor choice and another would be better, so I cut back still further. Sometimes it happens that two shoots instead of one come out of a single cut; then I must take one off. If the rose is grafted, as many are, sucker stems can sprout and begin growing below the union. These must always be quickly cut out so as not to have two different roses growing in one spot.

When at last the slow procession culminates in unfolding petals—the "so many eyelids" of crimson, palest pinks, sunlit yellows, and their corresponding crimson, pink, or yellow scents— the gardener's experience of roses seems all the deeper for having followed each bud on its journey. But even then the pruning does not stop. Cutting a faded flower's stem back to a healthy leaf cluster brings new shoots, so picking is pruning too, and (except for a few types that have only a short season of bloom) it means there will be more flowers to pick. In climates where there is frost, gardeners must remember to stop cutting as summer ends; otherwise the new growth that results might not harden off in time for winter and so be killed by the frosts; death of new growth can hurt, sometimes kill, the whole plant. When roses are left to fade on the bush, they turn into hips and feed the birds.

Pruning trees

Once a gardener has pruned a cornflower, a lilac, and a rose, he or she may become interested in pruning a tree. All trees will live longer and grow more beautifully if their dead or damaged or overshadowed branches are cut out cleanly and properly. With small trees, such as hawthorns, dogwoods, and shadbush, gardeners might do this themselves when the trees are dormant in winter. A little red-handled Felco folding saw works very well for cutting out branches up to four inches. It is amazingly sharp, cuts smoothly, and allows one to get in close in tight places. For anything bigger, one needs a bow saw or a straight pruning saw. Any branch that is more than two inches thick should be taken out in two parts, otherwise its weight may cause the trunk to tear before the cut is complete. So one first cuts off the branch, leaving a stump about a foot long, then carefully and cleanly removes the stump with a cut close to the trunk but angled slightly outward.

Big trees should be left to a tree surgeon: climbing into a big oak or maple with a chain saw and felling heavy limbs, without hurting the tree or anything beneath, needs specialized training. Usually the only pruning that is needed is, again, removing dead or damaged branches; just the same it is a job that needs to be done with care and sensitivity. Paying a good tree surgeon to spend a day is certainly an expense, but one seldom needs this more than once every ten years, and few single days can make so dramatic a difference to the vitality and radiance of the whole garden.

Learning by doing: pruning an apple tree

Fruit trees are the archetypal garden plant. A garden with nothing but a single apple tree in it would still be a garden, since it would have flowers and sweet fruit, spreading branches to sit in or under. Trees bearing every kind of fruit grew in the Paradise garden, but perhaps ever since Eve bit the apple from the tree of knowledge humans have needed to work on these trees: grafting, training, selecting, and breeding till it is hard to tell where nature ends and horticulture begins. This I think is why, though fruit trees gone wild can have a rare beauty, they do not fully tell their stories, in fruit or in loveliness, until they are pruned.

Apple and pear trees are pruned late in winter when they stand black and bare on frozen ground. It is difficult then to imagine what one can possibly do to help them grow into the green leafiness, heavy with fruit and beauty, that one wants to see in August.

For a long time this was a mystery to me, and I let it remain that way, since I was married to an orchardist. Naturally, he did all the pruning in our garden. His apple trees were pure essence of tree. What he did seemed so magical—a concentrated flurry of snippings and sawings, resulting in a mountain of fallen branches and a suddenly revealed new tree, graceful, accessible, and resolutely fruitful—that it only slowly occurred to me that here was something I could learn myself.

I did learn, though, in the only sensible way—by tagging along, asking questions, and watching every move, until I had seen enough to try a tree of my own. There is always a method in pruning, and it is by watching a pruner's hand, while keeping in mind the idea he or she is working from, that one eventually catches the hang of it: the magic, while still magic, becomes also craft. I will try to project this experience onto these pages, beginning with the laws of growth that pruners inwardly review while they find their tools and check the blades for sharpness:

1. To form fruit, buds must have light. This means no branch should overshadow another. If one branch is directly above another, there must be at least three feet between them. The buds on top or on the side of a branch will be more fruitful than those underneath.

2. Vertical branches are less fruitful, horizontal branches more so. Orchardists often lightly weight a young branch, or tie it down, to increase its horizontality; the resulting change in angle will be enough to turn buds that would have only formed leaves into fruit buds.

3. Every tree wants to grow *up*. Therefore pruning to a central leader—a single, vertically tending trunk—is a method that

combines what every tree wants to do with what its pruner
needs it to do. Usually the upward movement in a tree concentrates itself in one terminal bud, which becomes one
central upright trunk. If, as often happens, that single bud is
damaged or pruned out, the upward movement of the trunk
becomes elaborated into many vertical trunks and many
vertical branches, forming a tree with a great deal of wood
and very little fruit. If the pruner can maintain or restore the
central leader, then the vertical movement of the tree will
remain concentrated at a single growing point. The tree is
happy: it is satisfying its desire to move up. The gardener is
happy too, because one vertical trunk will not interfere with
his or her access to the tree; neither will it overshadow its
own side branches. It will be a fine central point from which
will originate the strong horizontal branches that will bear
the crop.

4. No matter how a tree is pruned, it always has a form of its
own that it "wants" to keep and will return to, come what
may. The pruner must find that form and work with, rather
than against, it, or he or she will always be at war with the
tree.

Now I have my tools: my saw for large cuts, hand pruners for
working in close. They have to be sharp: a dull blade will produce
a jagged cut that can hurt the tree. To heal without injury or
infection a cut must be clean, made with a sharp blade and flush
with the branch from which it is taken, so as not to disturb the
flow of sap.

Armed with my tools and principles, I put on gloves, wool
sweater, and down jacket (most of which gear will be shed as I

warm to the work) and venture into the garden on a February morning with frost in the ground. The air is still and cold, but with a little spring damp in it, lively with expectancy. Though it is very much a winter tree I am going to prune—its branches bare and sharply outlined against the gray sky—a bare tree in late winter feels very different from one at the season's beginning. The buds have swollen, full of possibility. Still, I hesitate: so many choices to make. Then, reminding myself that in pruning, as in life, no step forward is ever taken without forgoing others, I cross the lawn.

The tree is a semidwarf cox orange pippin (an English apple that does well on Long Island) about eight years old and fifteen feet tall. Most of the branches—and there are very many—are concentrated between three and eight feet off the ground. Somewhere inside this incomprehensible thicket there must be a sensible tree unfolding a sensible form, but first it must be found.

I take a deep breath and walk a slow circle around the tree, remembering a fundamental pruning rule: don't prune one branch at a time. First prune the whole tree, then the branches. This means first find the central leader and the basic framework branches that define the structure of the tree.

After the fourth or fifth circumambulation, and some standing back, and some moving closer, I see that there is already a strong vertical trunk to the tree. The reason I did not perceive it at first is that it is surrounded by several vertical and nearly vertical shoots. My first task, therefore, is to remove all these interlopers, carefully sawing them out.

When this is done the shape of the tree is much easier to follow. Now I can find five horizontal branches that grow out of the center of the tree and look healthy and flexible. These are the framework branches. My next moves must be to protect these branches, to give them all the light and space they need. This means that I must now remove all the branches that are either overshadowing them from above or competing with them by coming too close or crossing over.

These first steps of pruning the whole tree are the defining ones. I spend more time looking and thinking than cutting. The cuts, when I make them, are large ones, made slowly and deliberately with the saw (remembering, first, to cut each branch to a stump, and then carefully and cleanly to saw the stump from the trunk).

The next stage is to work branch by branch. If a branch is too crowded and elaborated with forks and side branches, the fruit will not ripen. Here I am looking for branches that grow straight out of the trunk in one continuous graceful movement. I have to find or sometimes make them. When I find such a branch I favor it, by taking out any other branches that shade or cross it. When looking at a forked branch and deciding which side to take out, it is always the fork that is growing in a different direction from the main part of the branch that I cut. Other times I do not remove a branch completely, but only shorten it, "heading in" to a side shoot that will bear fruit without altering the structure of the branch. These cuts must always be made less than a quarter of an inch from the last bud on the branch.

I circle the tree, doing this to every branch, working with my hand pruners. Sometimes I thin every fork on the branch only to discover at the end that the whole branch should be cut out, but I would not have known that till I thinned. It can be difficult at first to see what a branch is really trying to do. I must concentrate and look hard. My decisions become the accumulation of a thousand tiny messages from the tree; some I can consciously observe, others feel more like a growing sympathy.

The next step is detailing. I go around yet again, by now almost dizzy. This time the job is to remove new suckers (vertical branches, always barren) a few inches long, to cut out small forks, and to thin out the fruit spurs themselves, favoring the plump healthy buds over the thin peaked ones, and spurs above the branches over those beneath. This last stage has direct bearing on the fruit itself. As I reduce the number of potential fruits, those that remain will be bigger and take on their proper shape and richest color. A commercial orchardist or a home gardener with a favorite tree will want to make sure that all the fruits that set will be the healthiest and best proportioned on the branch. One could spend hours on this stage. Or one could skip it altogether if one simply wants a healthy, well-shaped tree and some fruit for cooking.

I take a middle course with our cox, enough to feel I have met the fruit and secured some plump apples for the fall. With the tree thinned out, I can easily walk into its middle—something that will be important at apple-picking time. Now that I can reach it, I can also fine-tune the central leader itself, making sure there are no forks or competing leaders at the top.

With this work on the uppermost tip, the pruning is done. Now I can stand back and look again at the whole tree. Its branches spiral around its center in a gesture both upward and generous. Its form is a raised cup that the spring sunshine can fill with blossom and leaf, the summer's warmth with fruit. I am proud of it and concerned for its future. Will it thrive?

That depends. I have begun something I must continue. Pruning creates an expectancy. The tree will grow vigorously now, but if that new growth is not accompanied by other care, an imbalance might occur which could be harmful; the tree might exhaust its reserves. The soil around its roots should be kept cultivated, free of weeds and grass; I must feed it with compost in spring, watch for insect infestations, water it in summer droughts. But I will do all this gladly, for our association is close now, and happily begun.

Chapter 8 Flowers

Who would have thought my shrivelled heart
Could have recovered greenness? It was gone
   Quite underground; as flowers depart
To see their mother-root, when they have blown;
         Where they together
         All the hard weather,
   Dead to the world, keep house unknown.

George Herbert, "The Flower"

Rose, pure contradiction, joy
to be nobody's sleep under that many
eyelids.

The epitaph on Rainer Maria Rilke's grave, written by himself

*L*ike a smile—so quick and ephemeral one could doubt one saw it except that suddenly everything changed—flowers speak from out of nature's depth. Pick six blue cornflowers and a red zinnia and set them in a jam jar in a room; light gathers there, refracts. We take flowers to weddings, graves, altars, to the places where it would be sacrilege to bring anything more solid. Gardeners grow them.

Flowering is that moment between green leaf and ripening fruit when the plant communicates with the insect world. Once I saw a film, made with infrared photography, that showed what bees see when flying through a garden. Besides the seductive colors and forms that are visible to the human eye, every blossom is daubed with brilliant markings, dots and arrows vivid as road signs: THIS WAY! OVER HERE! directing pollinators to nectaries.

But the moment of flowering is also when plants connect in a singular way with human experience. We perceive the flowers through our senses: smell, sight, touch. Yet the pictures that develop are inner ones, emblems of the soul's journey. The old names tell the story: heart's ease, love-in-a-mist, forget-me-not, passion flower. Each flower makes its own gesture of shape and color, conveys its particular mood. Compare the innocent daisy to sinister monkshood, lupines to anemones, violets to dahlias, foxgloves to zinnias.

Flowers go beyond mood to universal principle. Consider the lilies of the field; then think of roses, which carry the weight of the eternal symbol from the great windows at Chartres and Notre-Dame to Rilke's cryptic epitaph and still remain fragile, fragrant, intimate, for they are more than symbols, carrying their stories in themselves.

Nothing evokes a particular place and time as flowers do. A friend who lives on an island in Maine sent me seeds from a pale poppy she grows in her garden. Every year when they flower in mine, rocks, spruces, even eagles rise up before my inner eye. My mother, exiled from Austria, re-created the Alps of her childhood in the tiny garden behind our house in London with harebells, wild strawberries, and a certain sunny cragginess. Now on eastern Long Island, gardening near the sea, I realize I am evoking that evocation. It all gets very complicated, and I am sure it always has and always should.

For all these reasons I cannot advocate color schemes for the garden, or decorating with flowers. Flowers engage the heart's affections and unlock the deepest associations. It would be presumptuous for anyone to recommend to anyone else what to plant. Each gardener will have or will find their own reasons for growing what they do. And the gardens that result will be richer, more fascinating, than any re-creation of Miss Jekyll's drifts.

This having been said, gardeners nonetheless need to become familiar with the ways and forms of the flowers they might want to grow. Their cultivation naturally varies with their habits, and so, in subtle ways, does their character. A look at how form and habit intertwine offers glimpses into the "house unknown."

Annuals, perennials, biennials

Garden flowers are broadly categorized by their growth cycles. There are the hardy annuals, those plants that accomplish their entire cycle of growth in one year, then fade and die. Tender annuals might be perennial in some places, but only live one summer in areas where there is frost. Perennials come back, but vary greatly as to how often. Some, even at their healthiest, live only three or four years. Others, if they are happy where they are, can live undisturbed for nearly a century.

Annuals float on slender stems and light leaves, airy in the summer breeze. Flowering is all. They are colorful, friendly, ephemeral. They propagate themselves primarily by seed, so setting seed is the whole focus of the plant. If one keeps cutting the flowers from an annual plant it will go on sending out more and more flowers, all determined to produce as much seed as possible. Calendulas and cosmos, for instance, will bloom from June to October, if they are planted in good soil, watered, and assiduously picked.

Perennials set seed too. But they also send much of their growing energy into the ground, where their roots gather strength for the winter ahead. The flowering season for perennials is often relatively short, sometimes only a few days, sometimes, rarely, as long as a month. Meanwhile the body of the plant, its stem and leaves, becomes much more substantial. In deep tones of many greens, the perennial plants bring mass, shape, and architecture to the garden. When at last they bloom, it happens slowly. Gardeners can watch each increment of unfolding: a stem of yellow iris flowers slides sideways out of a spear-shaped leaf, a crimson tree peony explodes petal by petal from its huge green bud.

It used to be a convention of formal gardening to keep annuals and perennials in separate beds. Few people do that now. My flower bed would look too sad to me in August if I did not plant mallows, larkspur, and tobacco plants to bloom among the dark leaves of the peonies, the vanishing lilies, and fading delphiniums. But the differences are there, like tempos in music—allegro, andante—and gardeners keep time.

I grow most of my annual flowers among the vegetables. I plant them in clumps at the corners of beds, in between the bean rows, and among the squash. The vegetable garden is a sensible place to grow annuals for several reasons. Vegetables need a lot of sun and so do most annuals. Then, like the vegetables, annuals are sown in spring, picked all summer, thrown onto the compost pile in autumn.

Gold calendulas and cobalt cornflowers shine like jewels

among dark spinach leaves, red-veined beet greens, basil, and leeks. They bring bees, dragonflies, butterflies. Finches swoop down for their seeds. And all this generous blossoming harmonizes beds that would otherwise be filled with only leaf and root.

Flower beds evolved because perennials grow best in a situation that has been prepared especially for them. They want to be allowed to put down roots in ground that is deeply dug and well manured. Every three or four years certain plants will need to be divided and renewed; others will simply grow, preferring not to be touched at all. Except for some gentle hand-weeding, they want to be left in peace.

There are many ways to make beds. Some people like to create small ones here and there to mark particular places—a rock, a bench, a door. Then too it sometimes happens that a part of the garden seems to call out for a particular plant. One edge of my garden is a bit damp and lies beneath tall oaks that are slow to leaf out, so there is sun in spring, green shade in summer. This is what lilies-of-the-valley love. By now nothing else grows there, and for two weeks in May the whole garden is filled with their scent.

But for the devoted plant-watcher there is nothing quite like the long, narrow border, two to five feet wide, filled with perennials (judiciously mixed with annuals). Here the gardener works with both space and time, becoming skilled at overlapping one season of bloom with another. Wandering along the edge of such a bed, one can meditate upon the whole spectrum of growth and decay, noting on a single morning that the oriental poppies have gone to seed and their leaves are yellow and withering, the pink shoots of the platycodon have only just broken through the earth, and the rose is in bloom.

Biennial flowers follow still another rhythm. They form leafy growth in their first year but need a whole winter underground before they can return the following spring to flower, set seed, and die. So to cultivate biennials one must nurture tiny plants through a whole growing season, keep track of them over winter, transplant them in spring, all for one brief season of bloom. Why would anyone bother?

Only because among the biennials are some of the most poignant of garden flowers. Hollyhocks are biennial; so are Canterbury bells, deep blue, pale blue, shell pink, and white, their big bell-shaped blossoms so finely articulated one can almost hear them ring. Wallflowers come in strange colors. Imagine a dark brown flower. But their scent in early spring is like poetry. There are some perennial foxgloves, but the ones with towering spikes and mysterious purple freckles are biennial, as are sweet williams, English daisies, and Iceland poppies.

Naturally there are gardeners who feel that they cannot do without one or several of these, so they persevere. It is really not so bad. A good way is to occupy a small corner of the vegetable garden for a seedbed. The lightly shaded end where one would grow summer lettuce is best. Most biennials need to be sown in June or July. If one will be watering and weeding beans and tomatoes, then tending a few foxglove seedlings close by will not take much extra effort. Mark them well before winter.

When spring comes they will be ready to move to the flower bed. (Hollyhocks are an exception; they have long taproots and have to be moved into place the summer before, when they are still very small.) One chooses an overcast day, perhaps with a light rain falling, and, with a big enough trowel, scoops them out and carries them to their predug holes. They are seldom any trouble.

Then one has only to wait for the flower buds to form and beautifully unfold.

In formal gardens the biennials are pulled out as soon as they have finished their bloom to make room for something else, perhaps autumn chrysanthemums. Sensible gardeners leave them where they are to set seed and make new plants for the year to come.

The year marked by flowers

Many gardeners discover in themselves a quiet determination to have *something* in bloom in their gardens for as many months in the year as the weather will allow. This is for beauty of course, and because a plant in flower, even if it is a solitary frost-bitten calendula, focuses the garden and gives direction to daily wanderings. But I think it is also because flowers mark the passage of time. Not every flower, but certain particular ones, in their shape or color or scent, distill the innermost essence of the season. They tell us where in the year we are.

My smallest son in a woolen hat hurries into the kitchen to tell me he has found the first snowdrop. His excitement comes in part from the flower, but also it is because he is telling me that even though there is ice on the puddles, spring is really coming. He knows because it happens like this every year, but I think that even if he had never seen one before, the snowdrop's sudden wake-up bell of white petals with green rims would tell him.

Where I live, the time-markers of early spring are pale yellow daffodils and primroses that mirror the soft April sunlight that filters through clouds and bare branches. In June, when summer begins, a friend with a one-roomed house built into a bank in the woods gives a laurel-watching party. His garden is the somber forest itself and we sit on the terrace and watch it light up with the floating blossoms and wafting scent of opening mountain laurel. Autumn time-markers are not white chrysanthemums, which seem too pristine for that fecund season, but the fire-colored ones with flame-shaped petals, and purple Michaelmas daisies and red Chinese lanterns, all of them images of ripeness, glowing through fall's hazes and early dusks.

Finding the flowers that tell the story of the cycling year is something one can do only slowly. One needs to get to know the moods of the seasons where one lives, their particular slants of light, the changing quality of air. The flowers tell about the season, and the seasons send one looking for the flower, in neighbors' gardens, and nurseries, plant books, and sometimes memory. Like children learning to speak, gardeners acquire a subtle vocabulary of plants almost without thinking about it, simply because there is so much that needs to be said.

SPRING BULBS

Most of the first spring flowers are bulbs. Unless there is a very good garden shop nearby, there is more to be learned by ordering bulbs by mail from a thick catalogue (Dutch Gardens of Lisse-Holland via Adelphia, New Jersey, is a reliable and reasonably priced one). One can almost always get the basic spring bulbs—yellow daffodils (February Gold for the earliest flowers, reliable King Alfred for later), snowdrops, crocuses, and hyacinths—locally in nurseries or hardware stores. I like to rummage through bulb bins feeling for the fattest, firmest ones. But it would be a pity to be limited to these choices.

Winter aconites are golden yellow and shiny. As early as snowdrops, they make tiny suns against the melting snow. The first crocuses to bloom are not the bright "mammoth" varieties but the smaller snow crocuses, which have pearl-like colors—pale lilacs and creamy whites with golden centers. If one plants the mammoths as well, there will be about six weeks of crocuses. *Iris reticulata* are perfectly formed irises only three inches tall, that come out with the crocuses. Most commonly these are purple or yellow, but there is also a lovely pale blue variety with a yellow center (Cantab) that is very vernal. Later on come checked purple and white fritillaries called snake's head lily, and dog's tooth violet, which is not really a violet but has birdlike yellow flowers with recurved petals poised on tall stems; the bulbs are shaped like bones.

The crown imperial is another fritillary, a huge bulb that can cost four dollars for just one, but one is enough for most gardens. Three or four feet tall with a crown of orange or yellow florets under a tuft of green, it looks like an imperial scepter and used to be carried in front of English May Day processions, next to the Green Man. The bulbs themselves are extraordinary to contemplate—segmented, hollow at the center and with a musky smell more like that of a wild animal than a plant. They bloom around the first of May and when they do, it is important to crouch beneath the blossom and look up; within each floret hangs a shining pearl.

The best narcissus is a late one. Poet's narcissi are soft, six-petaled white stars with small, red-gold cups at their center. They sway on slender stems, giving off a scent that pierces the soul and stirs a nostalgia so strong it is hard to tell if it is for the past or the future. This is the reason for their name. There are two common varieties: Pheasant's Eye and Actaea.

None of these bulbs need to be planted in the flower bed at all. Most spring bulbs thrive in clumps around the lawn, or here and there between bushes and under trees. I planted most of mine with the help of small children, who dug holes wherever it struck their fancy. This looked a little arbitrary at first, but we were always stumbling on surprises, and now that the bulbs have settled in and multiplied, the whole garden looks like a glade in a medieval tapestry where the flowers spring up beneath the unicorn's feet.

Many kinds of bulbs will naturalize—return and multiply each year—if they are given room (another reason to plant them outside the flower bed). It is necessary to wait to cut back their leaves until they start to decay, and it is helpful to plant them deeply enough, with some compost and bone meal if the soil is poor. All the bulbs I have mentioned will return and multiply each year for several years. But one needs to be careful to choose varieties of daffodils and narcissus that specify on their box labels or catalogue description that they will naturalize, because some varieties do not. The crown imperials are temperamental, so one cannot count on them every year, and snowdrops spread by self-seeding, not by division, so they are chancy, sometimes spreading spectacularly and sometimes not at all.

RETURNS OF SPRING

A perennial bed in early spring is one of gardening's great revelations. Every day, among the dead stems of last year, new green tendrils and deep pink shoots make their mysterious, powerful appearances against the bare moist earth, unfolding and stretching into the light. Some of the new shoots will not get around to flowering for several months; others will mature and flower miraculously quickly.

Of the early-blooming perennials, the ones I love best are those whose blossoms echo the colors of tender sprouting—the purple pasqueflowers, with petals covered in a mist of fine hairs, pale yellow cup-and-saucer prim-  roses, sky-blue forget-me-nots, English daisies, then columbines, the shy "granny's bonnet" type, pink and blue, that lean down, and the taller long-spurred pale rainbow-colored ones that face up and seem ready to fly away, like tethered butterflies. (The granny's bonnets reseed, mix their colors, and spread; the long-spurred kind are hybrids and do not.)

Unlike herbaceous peonies, which die down to the ground, tree peonies develop gnarly wood stems that stay all year, growing eventually to four and five feet tall, bare and dramatic in winter beds. In early spring the austere woody trunks suddenly sprout beautiful, jagged leaves in greeny-red that embrace green buds that swell to an almost alarming size, then open slowly, petal by petal, finally revealing silky flowers often ten inches across, breathtaking in early morning fog. They finish their bloom just as the herbaceous peonies of late spring begin to bud. These were sacred plants kept in temple gardens in Tibet. One would think them beyond the reach of the backyard gardener, but I bought mine in a packet at Agway (a regional farm and garden supply store) for $4.95, a dead-looking twig with a root.

As the trees leaf out, casting the first green shade of the year, violets and lilies of the valley begin to open, and lilacs. These are the flowers of May and of romantic love. Once they are planted in the garden, they do not go away, just as certain experiences in the heart surprise us by their sudden recurrence when we thought we had forgotten. Gardeners who do not want such surprises had better not grow these flowers, but that is perhaps like saying they had better avoid that moment of spring.

Violets escape from flower beds and wander through the grass; lilies of the valley spread out under the trees. Near where I live there is a lilac bush that blooms year after year beside an old stone foundation in the woods. The people are gone, the house is gone, but the lilac still blooms.

THE MIDSUMMER GARDEN

The June-flowering perennial plants have something archetypal about them since their growth follows the sun's climb through the sky. They break through the earth soon after the equinox and reach their climactic moment of flowering on the longest day. I never understood midsummer until I started to garden. How could summer reach its height when it has barely begun?

From March to June there is a shine, an uprightness to each shoot that pokes through the earth, every green stem, leaf, and radiant blossom. When the solstice comes, the flowers in their beds seem to stand on tiptoe to greet the sun in the highest point in the sky. As soon as the solstice is passed—sometimes, I think, the very next day—the plants let go. Stems bend; the blossoms hang their heads and loosen their petals. One runs for the bamboo stakes to tie them up, but the plants have turned inward in a new gesture: time to form fruit. Plants that flower in June are too many to count, but growing the tall ones—foxgloves, delphiniums, hollyhocks, bearded iris, peach-leaved bellflowers—is a sure way to experience this gravity-defying climb toward the sun.

ROSES

Then come the roses:

> And in that rose you may well see
> Heaven and earth in little space
> *Res miranda!*

I should say that every garden should have at least one rose, but I know that I would need four, so as to have one of every color. The heavy-petaled, deep-scented crimsons seem to have most to do with ripening summer, but the old white rugosa rose Blanc Double de Courbet cools the garden and its light, pervasive smell is as fresh and innocent as Crimson Glory's perfume is resonant and sensual. No experience of sunlight is quite like the sight of light passing through yellow rose petals on a summer evening, and pink roses make me think of the warm faces of small children on their morning pillows, opening their eyes. So perhaps one rose is impossible: if one can grow roses at all, there might have to be four.

As to what kinds of rose—hybrid tea, antique shrub, rambler, climber—and which of the hundreds of available varieties (if one lives far north the choices will be fewer) to grow, the only answer is: the ones that grow well in one's own garden. One can ask the neighbors and study rose books, but ultimately the only way to find the right rose is to try them out. Gardeners can have a miserable time with roses—black spot, rust, aphid infestations—or they can have no trouble at all and find plants like my friend's Heritage which inexplicably grew to the size of a small shed.

If I have to struggle year after year with invisible worms, I usually decide it is the wrong rose. I have planted thirteen roses in my garden over the years. Four have died and I have pulled out three; six are thriving, with only weeding, pruning, and manure. This may have been a wasteful way to choose roses, but I do not know a better one, except that if I were starting again, I think would improve the odds by planting mostly David Austin's modern shrub roses (my friend's colossal Heritage is one of these; in my garden it does beautifully too, though it is nowhere near as big) that are now widely available. These have been specially bred for vigor and disease resistance, which is what makes them modern, while maintaining all the lyrical qualities of their fussier ancestors.

Roses must have at least six hours of sun and be planted with plenty of composted manure and perhaps a fish head under their roots. They must be watered well, but the water should go to their roots, not their leaves. Leaves that stay wet are a primary cause of fungus diseases, so when it is possible, it is always better to water roses in the morning, when the sun will quickly soak up the wetness, than in the evening. Rose gardens are not usually a good idea, because if a fungus disease or insect infestation strikes one rose, it is likely to spread to another. Far better than a rose garden is to find the rose or roses one loves. Then give each one an honored place with space to expand, shelter, and light breezes. It should be a spot one will often pass, so as to be reminded that summer is here.

FLOWERS OF SUMMER

Phlox, lilies, monkshood (which is very poisonous), purple cone-
flowers, bee balm, red and yellow yarrow, hibiscus, indigo harebells and Chinese bellflowers, and many others (but these are the
ones with deep summer colors) all flower in July and August. Still,
tending them is a very different experience
from caring for the flowers of spring: no
longer Edenic, for now one is struggling
with weeds and drought. After midsummer,
one shovels on more compost, both to feed the
plants and to cool the roots. Cutting off the stems
of fading June flowers will let the plants regain
strength and send up new leaves for a rich background to the summer flowers and often, in
autumn, a second flowering.

The annuals follow a different rhythm. Midsummer is often
when they are just beginning to flower. Pinching the flower buds
(this means snipping off the top bud when the plant has developed three or four sets of leaves) creates a bushy plant with strong
side branches and lots of flowers all around. This works well with
snapdragons, marigolds, cornflowers, and many others. Flowers all
around are the whole point of annuals. And the bees, dragonflies,
and butterflies that hover about them seem to extend the blooming further into the summer air.

One can choose annuals more adventurously than perennials,
which will return whether one likes them or not. Packets of seeds
don't cost very much. Every year I try something that sounds odd
or lovely in the seed catalogue, toadflax, maybe, or mignonette. If
I do not like them, at least I have learned something and it will

not come back next year. Or if an annual I like catches my eye in the nursery, I can buy a packet of six plants for two dollars.

But every year I grow my favorites: yellow and orange calendulas—their day's-eye faces like the summer sun, pink and white mallows, which are a kind of simple hollyhock that grows into a little bush instead of straight up, spires of purple larkspur, blue cornflowers the color of the summer sky with long silvery leaves. Love-in-a-mist is a paler, more crystalline blue, and floats in clouds of wispy foliage; later on the flowers turn into hairy little spheres, seedpods.

If I forgot to plant any of these, they would come back by themselves. I wonder if it is a coincidence that all my favorite annuals are hardy where I live. The seeds that fall to the ground in summer and autumn live through the winter underground and sprout when they are ready in spring, growing into well-anchored, robust plants. Perhaps that is why I like them. Or is it that annuals look most beautiful, most like themselves, under the skies where they belong? If I lived farther south where the light was more intense would I grow dahlias, zinnias, and African marigolds instead?

In spite of the brave annuals and the late-blooming perennials there comes a time, around the middle of August, when the whole garden seems exhausted. Leaves yellow, flowers fade; beetles prey upon the plants' fatigued state. Only the weeds thrive, and giant hibiscus and mammoth Russian sunflowers. This is the time to let things go, allow the weeds to run riot for a while and the flowers to go to seed, since they so much want to. One can pull a chair into the shade and read a book, or put the book down and watch the birds. There might be a goldfinch in the cosmos or a blue jay hanging from a sunflower, devouring seeds where the petals have fallen.

AUTUMN INTO WINTER

As the autumnal equinox approaches, the garden comes back to life. Now there is moisture in the air, and with each dip of the temperature toward frost, fresh flowers emerge with a new radiance. Zinnias and cornflowers sing in the clear light. This is when the June perennials, delphiniums and campanulas, send out their second flowering, not in a spectacular show like their first, but as a sweet recapitulation of a major theme, poignant among leaves that may have already been grazed by frost and turned a vermilion red. The roses return, but one should try not to pick them, as cutting encourages new growth which would be killed by frost, hurting the plant. Instead one just watches as they bud and open, fade and form hips.

Each frosty morning one goes out to see what has survived among the ruins. As the dahlias turn black, unearthly silver-pink windflowers—Japanese anemones—open up beside them. Chrysanthemums turn deeper russet, orange, and red. Michaelmas daisies spread like weeds, casting a blue and purple haze over the flower bed. Frost strikes the low spots first. In sheltered niches among the bean poles or against a wall a few flowers hang on. Will there be calendulas on the Thanksgiving table? A single Crimson Glory rose?

In my garden the last stragglers are gone around the winter solstice. I can expect the first snowdrop toward the middle of

February. In between is a pause, but it is not as if nothing is happening. There is an old custom of burying the seeds saved for spring planting between December twenty-fourth and January sixth, when they are taken up again. These are the "holy nights," the twelve longest of the year. Modern seed-savers know about stratifying certain seeds and put them in the refrigerator for a few days, but this could not be quite the same. After the coldest nights, frost flowers appear on the window. Contemplating these, gardeners ponder what might be happening underground when nothing intervenes between earth and bright winter stars.

Chapter 9 *Vegetables*

Harvest moon—
called at his house,
   he was digging potatoes.

Buson

*R*eviewing the history of gardening, one sees that turnips seldom grew in gardens designed for contemplation and delight. In the gardens of Renaissance villas, Buddhist temples, or English country houses, kitchen plots were hidden behind walls and hedges. It was as if, in feeding their souls, contemplatives and aesthetes avoided reminders of their bodies' humble needs. John Blofield, one of the few Westerners to have visited the ethereal, mountaintop gardens of Taoist hermitages in prerevolutionary China, recalled, "Vegetable gardens must have existed though I cannot recall having seen more than one or two; perhaps they were hidden away, their appearance being too humdrum for the vicinity of immortals reputed to live on sups of wind and sips of dew."

Things are different at the end of the second millennium. Daily life flickers dimly on a screen, or through the tinted glass of a windshield. Friends and lovers keep "in touch" by telephone; dinner is summoned with a fax. Souls ache with chronic disembodiment. In the garden, though, beets and carrots grow. Their leaves expand in the sun and roots explore among the pebbles and worms of the soil. Gardeners in thick sweaters sit on sheltered benches in pale sunlight and eat their first spring sandwiches— maybe bread and cheese with lettuce thinnings, slices of radish, a few chives—very slowly, remembering the roots of existence.

Without vegetables there could be a serene emptiness at the heart of my garden, the open center recommended by the great landscape designers. As it happens, the geographic center of my garden is the only place where sun falls unshadowed for most of the day, a requirement for most vegetables. So the lawn makes its green way around a rough circle of vegetable beds segmented by narrow paths. In summer tomato plants, bush beans, and chamomile tumble out of the edges and onto the grass.

In winter the beds are mostly empty, some mulched with sea- weed, some with salt hay, some bare. Only a few deer-chewed stalks of blue kale and some clumps of withered leeks stand out. In early spring half the beds still linger in winter sleep and rumpled mulch. The others have been woken one by one with rake and seeds, and, after the first spring rain, a green haze of seedlings hov- ers over black soil. I go on planting turnips and peas even as there are fewer people around to eat them and it would be cheaper to go to the store.

Virtues of farms, virtues of gardens

Fifty, even twenty, years ago lots of gardeners grew lots of vegeta- bles. This is becoming much rarer. Because today's economy demands long hours of work away from home, a big vegetable garden becomes, paradoxically, "impractical." But a small garden that is loved can grow food that is medicine for blunted senses— finely formed, sharply flavored, fragrant. Even a little of this kind of nourishment goes far.

Because most vegetables are annuals that must grow from seed to maturity in a matter of weeks, they need more sun, richer soil, and closer cultivation than perennial plants. A lettuce or carrot that has developed too slowly, starved of sun or good soil, or strangled by weeds, will never arrive at the flavor and shape that really belong to it. Therefore one can only grow as many vegetables as one has time, good soil, and sunny space for. Perhaps this is not very many, but it may not matter.

I started growing vegetables with a sense of grim necessity. It was the time of *Silent Spring*. Twenty years ago I saw fat geese browse on weeds at the edge of a nearby potato field, then keel over and die before the spray wagon was back in the barn. The potatoes and beans that I could buy in the shops, even if grown far away, were probably treated with the same insecticides. With a baby at home, I decided that it would be better to grow my own.

I learned a lot about vegetables in those years, but never how to feed a family. I loved the variety of what I could grow and we could eat: beyond carrots and spinach came salsify and black radishes, buttercup squash, muskmelon. I discovered what a cucumber flower looks like, how an onion bulb grows from a seed. The quantities were what defeated me: too many beans, not enough carrots, no room for corn; famine and waste side by side.

Fortunately for everyone, time was on our side. A few of the new generation of farmers where I live gave up wholesaling potatoes to become expert market gardeners, growing organic vegetables to sell at their own stands or truck to greenmarkets in the city. With compost, courage, imagination (and often their own young children to think about), the new farmers began the slow transformation of their fields. Birds sang in the hedgerows, and we could gratefully buy good vegetables.

After those years of effort, I will never take our food for granted. Nor can I: the economics of these new farms and their associated greenmarkets and food co-ops are still precarious. They need devoted customers, and I am one. But I still plant my garden. Gardens and farms complement one another, but they are not the same.

Farms have sunny fields, tractors, greenhouses, and professionalism. The life of a farmer turns around the timing of the crops. Gardens tend to follow the vicissitudes of a gardener's life. From the farm, therefore, issue sacks of carrots, cabbages, and parsnips, bushels of winter squash, potatoes, and yams—whatever is thick-skinned, stalwart, and rooty will keep in the refrigerator, cellar, or cool pantry. I can grow all these things, but never enough of them and, often, not as well. So once a week in summer, I go shopping at farm stands, and in the fall I stock up for winter.

But as a source of what is delicate and green, fragrant and ephemeral, nothing can compare with a garden. Just as ripeness is all in a parsnip or a pear, almost the whole value of some crops is in their fleeting freshness. The time to pick young string beans is when the water to cook them in is already boiling. One harvests the salad leaves when the table is set and the birds are flying home in the twilight. I seldom manage to serve peas for dinner, because the children eat them all in the garden, standing by the vines and grazing.

Vegetables are truly domestic. It is not just that cooks like to have them close at hand so they can pick them near the kitchen door. It is also that vegetables love to grow there: they thrive as part of the larger community of the home garden. Hedges, trees, fences, and the walls of houses give shelter from rough winds. If the air is full of the scents of flowers and herbs, bees for pollination and good wasps will be drawn. Bushes and trees are nesting places for birds that control insect infestations.

When I began growing vegetables, I worried about how to give all the different vegetables their separate requirements. The books I read told me they needed such various soils. Cabbage thrives in dank, clay soil, spinach needs a sandy, light-filled one. Swiss chard likes a sweet soil; tomatoes and peppers want a little acidity. How could I sort all this out in one small plot?

It is true that each plant family—and subgroup within it—has its unique cultural needs, and it is helpful to know what they are. But a little garden—unlike a farm—can, without huge effort, be worked entirely by hand, kept well supplied with compost and soil preparations, rested and rotated.* A garden soil can thus be so enlivened, balanced, and rich in humus that it will give most vegetables the wherewithal to find what they need.

---

*If one is growing vegetables in beds, planting in rotations is not difficult to manage, although a bit like a slow puzzle. The important thing is to keep notes and a map in one's garden journal to remember what went before. In the simplest kind of rotation, one just tries to make sure not to repeatedly plant vegetables from the same family in the same bed. A good vegetable book will tell which vegetable is related to which, which is not always obvious. It will say which plants are the heavy feeders—for example, lettuce, spinach, and corn. And it will lay out which make light demands—carrots, beets, radishes—and which actually help feed the soil, like peas and beans and cover crops such as alfalfa and clover. One then takes care to follow heavy feeders with crops that will deplete the soil only a little or even renew it, and vice versa. If one can manage it, it is good to also think about following leafy, shallow-rooted crops with deep-rooted ones, roots with flowers, and so on, thereby keeping the soil lively with change.

Another reason why vegetables flourish in home gardens is diversity itself. Many plants grow better in community with different but sympathetic plants (as they tend to grow in nature) than they would lined up alone in a field. Some affinities between plants are mechanical in nature: deep-rooted carrots aerating the soil for shallow-rooted lettuces, tall corn plants shading and cooling winter squash plants in the summer heat. Other happy companionships are more mysterious, originating in root secretions, or exchanges of fungi, or subtle exhalations from leaves or flowers. Most of these relationships have been observed rather than explained and have been passed along from gardener to gardener. "Turnips like peas, potatoes like beans." And some plants really do dislike one another and stunt each other's growth. Primers of companion planting (I like *Companion Plants and How to Use Them* by Helen Philbrick and Richard Gregg) are valuable tools, but so are a gardener's own observations.

Design of vegetable gardens

A garden grown for freshness looks quite different from one in which quantities of vegetables are grown to ripen all at once and store. In the latter the garden will be dug all at one time, perhaps planted in rows for ease of cultivation with a wheeled hoe or tiller. It will look a bit like a miniature farm. In a garden grown for frequent harvests—meal by meal—small sowings are made often, so there will always be something young and tender just coming on. In this sort of garden small beds are more sensible.

The beds are hand dug at the outset (see chapter 2), but one can do this little by little. Once they are established, they are raked over and replanted bit by bit as needed. Gardeners who are not sure how much they can manage can begin with one or two tiny beds, adding more only if they become enthusiastic. Because they are never walked on, beds should only be as wide as can easily be reached into from one side or another to harvest plants or to thin or weed. This dimension will vary with the length of the gardener's arms or that of the gardener's smallest assistant. Four feet is a good average; then one is never more than two feet away from the farthest radish.

The shapes and configurations of the beds can be whatever fits into the contours of the garden, faces the sun, and strikes the gardener's sense of place. It intrigues me to see how few good vegetable gardens resemble each other. Each one has something unique and beautiful about its layout. I think this is because the best gardeners respond to precisely where they are.

My own vegetable garden is round: a circular bed for perennial herbs, surrounded by concentric circle segments for the rotating vegetables. To skeptical visitors who asked if I was making a flower clock, I primly replied that a round vegetable garden was the most efficient use of what sunny space I had. But the truth is that, in a vegetable garden, beauty and practicality are seldom separate issues, and my circle looked lovely to me.

The paths between beds must be wide enough to be walked through and sat in, and to push a mower through if they are grass. My paths are grass and clover, because this is inviting and pleasant under bare feet. But I have to be strict about edging with a sharp spade or the grass invades the beds. (And for a couple of weeks in summer when the clover is in bloom, I have to be careful not to step on bees.) Some people make nice paths of mulch or wood chips. And I have even seen them laid out in brick or stone where gardeners are very sure of their design.

Vegetables grown in beds thrive if interplanted in sympathetic communities, following guidelines of companion planting, the distribution of helpful herbs and flowers, and the growing of "catch crops" (fast-growing vegetables filling the spaces between slower ones, spaces that might otherwise be filled by weeds). So spinach grows up between peas, young lettuce among garlic shoots, a thyme plant here, a yarrow there, edgings of chamomile or savory. Golden calendula flowers shine among leaves of purple mustard. A garden grown for freshness looks like a garden.

Time in the vegetable garden

Besides fitting easily into the garden space, growing vegetables for freshness can also fit nicely into the hours of a gardener's life. Planting small crops often—being a little engaged with the vegetables over a long period rather than intensely busy for a shorter one—means gardening in small increments of time, which these days are often all a person has. An hour before work with dew on the ground and green leaves translucent in the long rays of dawn, half an hour while a baby naps in the afternoon, twenty minutes after dinner as colors fade into dusk. Such brief interludes can be all that is needed for there to be something to pick for supper, month after month. They can also redeem the whole day.

Planting small crops often—succession planting, as it is called—

naturally works best if the growing season is long. But whatever the seasonal boundaries, gardeners can usually find ways to extend them (see chapter 4). This might mean gardening all year round where there is no frost, or for three months instead of five where the season is tightly squeezed between late last frosts and early first ones. The trick is in getting to know one's local weather and planting accordingly. A climate zone is one thing, but within that climate zone is the particular microclimate to which one's garden belongs. Then, within the garden itself, there might be a south-facing bed sheltered by a wall, in which spring could begin a month early, or a bed in the shade of a tree where bolt-resistant lettuce might survive the summer's heat. Good vegetable gardening depends on trying it out, being experimental at first, open to risk and mistakes, then canny.

Looking through my old gardening notebooks, I see how widely the dates of plantings and harvests in my garden have varied from year to year with shifts in weather, or sometimes with disturbances in my life. But though the dates vary, the sequence is always the same. Choosing planting times is never so much a matter of dates on the calendar as it is of becoming familiar with the way one event coincides with or follows another. It is the pattern that remains the same. So I can plant beans when the lilacs bloom, but some years that might be during the first week in May and some years not till the last.

Usually, the successions in my garden take place over rather a long season. I might begin in March, if the winter is mild and I am ready, and harvest until December, if the hard frosts keep off. But in a cold wet spring I might not plant till almost May, and sometimes a cold snap in October kills everything but the kale. Still, the sequence remains essentially the same and would whether the season lasted four months or ten. Therefore I will trace it here in a kind of vegetable chronology.

A vegetable chronology

What follows is far from a complete list of vegetables. I will leave out zucchini, eggplants, potatoes, and many other vegetables a gardener might very well decide to plant because they love them, because they are curious about how they grow, or because the whole plant is an icon of the place and season (around here such a plant would be corn, which some people grow in village gardens just to watch it grow, though they only get half a dozen ears to eat). It is true that every year I grow at least one or two crops for at least one or two of those reasons—broad beans to remind me of my English childhood, salsify because I can't buy it, popcorn for my daughter. But the plants I have included in this calendar of vegetables are the ones I plant *every* year. The point of these plants—planted in these ways and this sequence—is that, when I grow them, I know that every day, from the first warm weeks of spring till the ground freezes hard in winter, there will be something fresh to pick.

SPRING GREENS

The first wild plants to sprout at winter's end are the bitter pungent ones: wild garlic, dandelion, watercress, nettle. The sulfurous juices that give these plants their sharp burning taste are the same elements that allow them to survive spring frosts. This is why the bitter greens are the first that can be planted, and probably the evolutionary reason why one craves their zest after the thick puddings and potatoes of winter. In the Grimms' "Rapunzel" a poor pregnant woman is driven to bargain away her unborn daughter by her burning desire for the salad greens growing in the garden of the witch next door. Rapunzelsalat is a green called corn salad, or mâche, that can grow with snow on the ground—I am quite sure the deal was made around the middle of March.

Spinach, mustard, turnip, arugula, and some lettuces—especially the "loose leaf" ones like Black-Seeded Simpson and Oak Leaf—can be planted in the garden as soon as the soil has thawed and fully dried out. If the weather keeps warming, there will be thinnings to eat about three weeks after planting, and real harvests as soon as five weeks. Most greens stay at their delicate primes for only two or three weeks; after that they toughen and grow bitter. So the rhythm for planting spring greens is to sow only as much at any one time as is likely to be eaten while the leaves are still young and sweet. I try to plant greens at least once a month. When possible I plant them when the moon is waxing, or at least when the air feels lively and I think it is going to rain. Sometimes I just plant them when I can.

The important thing is to get into the habit of continual small plantings, so one learns to make them quickly and well, without fuss. Then growing greens can become part of life. The bed is already there (having been dug five years ago, or the previous autumn, or at the very latest two weeks before, so that the soil has had a chance to settle down). To prepare the soil, all that is necessary is to skim the surface with a cultivator or sharp hoe to smooth it and dislodge potential weeds, scatter fine compost, then flatten the surface with a straight rake. Most seeds of greens—lettuce, arugula, mustard—are so small that there is no question of planting them in a particular configuration: one simply broadcasts the seeds, then covers them very lightly with sprinklings of fine soil, and pats them down. As the seedlings grow, one can thin them into the proper spacing (see chapter 4).

At a single planting, I might sow a quarter of a packet of arugula, half a packet of spinach, one of white and purple turnips (mostly for their leaves, but also for the turnips themselves—best picked small before the wireworms can get them), half a packet of Black-Seeded Simpson lettuce, some mustard greens. I plant a thin frontier of radish seeds between the spinach and the lettuce, a few larkspur seeds in corners and a border of calendula and cornflowers along the edge (to be pretty in summer). All of these together take up one half of a bed that is four feet by seven. As I go, I make little corner posts of twigs in the earth to map out what area is planted with what.

The whole procedure takes less than an hour. Then one can go back to what one was doing before—washing socks, finishing a chapter. A few days later, tiny green salad leaves appear. After three weeks, it is time to move on to the other half of the bed and plant again.

The first handful of fresh green leaves can transform any meal, beginning with bread and cheese at lunchtime. An austere supper of omelette and baked potato turns into an elegant dinner with the addition of a salad made of purple mustard, deep green spinach, and crimson radishes. When I can pick enough turnip greens to steam with oil and garlic and serve on spaghetti, we can taste that winter with its colds and infections is over at last.

GREENS FOR SUMMER

Later in spring, it is necessary to plan for the coming heat of summer. The delicate loose-leaved lettuces of spring will not survive in hot weather; neither will mustard or arugula. They bolt (rush to flower and form seeds) and become too coarse and bitter to eat. The lettuces that have the best chance to survive heat are the ones that turn themselves inward to form tight, blanched centers. These are the Bibbs and some romaines, and even these will need shade and frequent watering if the summer temperatures reach the nineties. Toward the end of spring I plant a Bibb called Butterhead, starting the seeds in a sunny seedbed, then I transplant them, when they are about two inches high, to another where there is afternoon shade. In August they make the coolest pale green salads all by themselves, with just oil and vinegar and a trace of sugar and salt.

Spinach will not grow at all in heat. But Swiss chard will, so I plant it in midspring to be ready for summer. Swiss chard grows into big plants, up to two feet tall with glossy green leaves with white veins (Fordhook Giant) or deep green leaves with crimson veins (Ruby Red). I mix the seeds of both because their complementary leaves look lush and lovely in the summer sun (in areas where there is late frost, the red should be planted a little later, as it is tenderer than the white). The seeds are spaced about three inches apart and eventually need to be thinned so that each plant has at least six inches of space all around it.

Swiss chard has to be thinned early because, as with beet seeds (chard is a kind of beet), each single bumpy "seed" is actually a shell holding several true seeds within it. Chard likes sweet soil, so it will usually do better if one sprinkles a little dolomitic lime right where the seeds will be planted.

Besides its beauty and nutritiousness, the great value of Swiss chard as a garden plant is that its leaves can be harvested week after week and month after month. Because it is biennial, it will not go to seed in summer as the annual summer greens do. As long as it has enough small young leaves near the stem on each plant to let it grow, water, and occasional compost, Swiss chard can be picked all summer and into autumn up to, and sometimes even beyond, the frost. This means an almost infinite source of fresh greens from a very small space.

The irony is that there are people—sometimes members of a gardener's own family—who will not eat this otherwise perfect vegetable because of its slightly claggy, bittersweet taste. When this happens one must not give up, but look for a better recipe. The one that usually changes people's mind involves steaming the chopped chard leaves just till they wilt, with a tablespoon of butter, and one each of soy sauce and honey, folded in among the leaves. Like all good recipes this one does not so much disguise the taste of the essential ingredient as make a virtue of it.

BEANS

Once the soil temperature has climbed to 60 degrees, or the point where the earth no longer feels chill to the touch, it is time to plant beans. Where I live the soil can reach 60 degrees a few weeks before the date of the average last frost, so planting early can be a little risky. I usually gamble—plant anyway, hoping for an early crop—and I usually win. A purple snap bean called Royalty is cold-resistant, so it is a good bean to start with. Three or four weeks later, I plant more beans, some bush, some pole, and I get beans all summer long.

Beans all summer long would be too many beans, if one grew only the ordinary green snap kind. But there are so many others. Purple beans (which grow out of pink flowers) end up green when cooked, and small children love to stand on a chair by the stove and watch them change. My favorite for taste are the flat Italian romano beans, like Jumbo. Yellow wax beans have a buttery flavor and vitamin A. I find new favorites all the time, the most recent being Dragons' Tongues, a wax bean that is pale green mottled with purple and delicious eaten young and tender or old and tough. A few aged Dragons' Tongues add intrigue and mysterious depth to soups made from light summer vegetables. All the above are bush beans.

Bush beans are easiest to cultivate if one grows them in short rows within a bed. I space my seeds four inches apart at a depth of twice their size and leave two feet between the rows. Beans are not demanding of soil, and in fact, being legumes, will leave it enriched with nitrogen. I set out sweet marjoram plants at the corners of my bean beds; it is supposed to make the beans more flavorful as they grow, and I always add a few leaves to the beans as they cook, for taste.

I began growing pole beans to combat the Mexican bean beetle. Mexican bean beetles are small, yellow, spiked beetles that in serious infestation will devour entire bean plants down to bare stems. I had them two years in a row and decided to try the recommendation frequently found in companion-planting manuals that potatoes grown with beans deter beetles. Since my space was small I attempted a two-story arrangement, planting a small crop of Green Mountain potatoes early in spring and then later on planting pole beans to rise above them. The beans did not seem to overshadow the potatoes unduly, and not one beetle came that year. I could not be sure if the potatoes had done it, or if the pole beans were more resistant than the bush beans, or if the beetles had moved on for their own reasons. But in any case, having got to know pole beans, I grew fond of them and have grown them ever since.

Pole beans take longer to mature than bush beans. In many gardens there is only time for one sowing, but one can plant some early and some late varieties and lengthen the season. I think that, because they grow more slowly, pole beans have deeper, more resonant flavor and coarser texture than most of their callower bush bean relatives. One can grow pole beans up vertical stakes, or in the tepees that small children really do like to sit in while their parent gardens nearby. Five or six seeds are set in a circle at the base of each stake. They need no other help in making their ascent. The poles must be dug a good nine inches into the ground or they will blow over in a wind. I have some thick bamboo stakes from a neighbor's garden; they are nine feet long, but even this does not go quite high enough. A foot or two of vines always blow in the breeze like summer flags, shaking their red, white, or purple blossoms and long green beans.

The key to maintaining a continuous supply of beans is to keep picking. As with annual flowers, if one allows the beans to ripen on the plant to the point where their pods are fat with seeds that are ready to drop, the plants will assume their job is done and begin to yellow and die. If the pods are picked while they are still young and tender, the plants will keep bearing for about two months. Some beans allow a gardener more latitude than others. At one extreme are the thin, elegant French filet beans that need constant attention. If one forgets to pick them for even thirty-six hours, they will become too stringy and tough to eat. (Anyone who has wondered why these beans are so expensive to buy will quickly understand if they grow their own.) At the other extreme are several leisurely pole beans that can be neglected for as long as a week and will keep patiently bearing, the lumpy pods still tender and tasty.

TOMATOES

When there is no more chance of frost, it is time to set out tomato plants. There is more lore about growing tomatoes than about any garden plant I know. I think this is because even after four hundred years of cultivation in the northern hemisphere, tomatoes still have an exotic, magic quality—their fruit so invitingly shiny and scarlet, yet a bit poisonous when green, their growth rampant and wild. Gardeners think they have to trick them into submission.

Tomatoes, unlike other garden plants, can thrive in their own debris. I grow mine in the same bed for several years. (If I had tomato pests or diseases I would move them, but this has not yet happened.) Too much manure will make tomatoes put out many leaves but not much fruit; a little is all right, mixed with half-rotted compost and perhaps some wood ash. The small plants need to be set deeply into the ground, a little at a slant, to grow strong roots. If several pairs of leaves have already formed, one can snip off all but the top pair and bury the stem: it will become root.

There are almost as many techniques for propping up tomato plants as there are gardeners, each as fallible as the gardener who employs it. I tie the main stems to thick posts with twist-'em wires as they grow, pruning out extra side-shoots all summer in an ongoing procedure. I always mulch the soil beneath with straw or grass clippings in case a branch or two bends to the ground despite my efforts. More dexterous gardeners surround their plants with little cages of wood or wire that work well for keeping their plants in bounds.

Some years I do not tie up my plants at all and they still produce plenty of fruit without much waste as long as I keep picking. The chief disadvantage I see in just letting tomato plants go free is that they take up much more room. A lying-down tomato plant needs an area about four feet by four feet, while one that is more or less standing up needs three by three. I am referring here to what are called indeterminate tomatoes, those that keep growing, on and on. Determinate tomato varieties are much tidier in their habit, and therefore need less space; however, since it is also in their nature to ripen all their fruit at once (good for canning), they do not strictly speaking belong on a list of plants for gardens grown for freshness.

Varieties of indeterminate tomatoes vary a great deal in the time they take to ripen, so one can get long harvests by planting combinations of early- and late-ripening varieties. Paying attention to tomato varieties is important. One of the main reasons to grow tomatoes in the garden is to cultivate the kinds one likes best. Buying started plants means less choice. But one can still search for favorites. Among the plants easily found at farm stands and garden centers, I look for Marglobe and Rutgers, nice medium size, with strong tomato flavor and summery tomato scent. For those willing and able to start plants from seeds, the possibilities are of course much wider. My current favorite is Moskvich, very early ripening, dark red, and beautifully round, sweet as the fruit they actually are. I order the seeds from Johnny's Seeds in Maine, which in turn obtained them from a grower in eastern Siberia, quite a journey for a plant that originated in Peru.

Seeds of tender basil can be sown at the same time that the tomato plants are set out. In fact, I like to plant it in between the tomato plants. Basil is a good companion for tomato in the ground as well as on a salad plate, and the toasty smell of warm tomato plant in the sun blends exquisitely with the piercing perfume of basil in the warm summer air.

GREENS FOR AUTUMN

Planting slows down in the heat of summer. Though corn, beans, squash, and other heat-loving plants grow well in temperatures over 80 degrees, many of the tender plants I grow for freshness either do not germinate or, if they do sprout, have trouble staying alive. Though I generally stop planting from the end of June till the middle of August, I make an exception for kale. Kale that will have the vigor and sweetness for autumn harvests (which spring-planted kale that has struggled through a hot summer will not) needs to be planted a few weeks before the first frost, not because the frost will hurt it, but because it needs long days in which to mature.

Farmers start their kale in flats in lath-covered greenhouses to keep it cool. Few gardeners have the patience to work with flats in summer. I seed my kale directly in a bed with my best compost and nurse it tenderly, keeping the soil well watered, lightly misting the leaves on very hot days. There is no known cure for flea beetles, which sometimes completely devour young seedlings. But if one has the willpower, one can plant again about three weeks later, by which time the beetles will have moved on and the kale will grow.

The reason to go through all this trouble is that kale can actually be picked and be delicious with snow on it. Gardeners who live where it does not snow have other choices for winter greens, but they might still consider kale for its extraordinary concentration of vitamins C and A. It is the perfect vegetable for short, dark days. Some people have been turned against it by eating kale that is overcooked, at which point it tastes like burnt rubber. But lightly steamed just until the green color becomes brilliant, or tossed in oil on top of a mixture of stir-fried vegetables, kale is a true delicacy. It is also the key ingredient in kale-and-potato soup, excellent with or without sausage on a cold night. With its blue-green or purple leaves it looks lovely still growing in the garden in the winter light.

As autumn approaches, the days are cool enough to plant lettuce again, also arugula and spinach. The leaf lettuces and romaines can survive a few light frosts. At dawn their leaves might be white and stiff, all sheathed in frost, but if the sun comes out they will be green and fresh at lunchtime. If young spinach meets a hard frost, it will often go quiescent over winter, then start growing again the following spring. If, however, the hard frosts happen to blow past the garden, there will be fresh green salads at Thanksgiving dinner.

A FEW ROOTS

Although it is not always practical, and I can never grow very many, I like to combine these small, quick plantings of vegetables grown for freshness with perhaps half a bed of more long-term, root vegetables that I start in early spring and do not harvest till fall or even winter. Some years, it might be a few rows of potatoes, Green Mountains, or Yellow Finns; another year half a bed of parsnips (which are at their best harvested during midwinter thaws when their sweetness is distilled). Most often—every year I can possibly manage it—I grow leeks (King Richard), seeding them outside in March and laboriously thinning and weeding them over the six months they take to mature.

My gardener's instinct likes to balance the fast-growing leafy plants with the slow, tuberous, bulbous, and rooty. My cook's experience tells me that whereas I cannot grow enough potatoes or leeks or parsnips to make frequent meals of them (I go to the farms for that), a cache of hoarded leeks, parsnips, or our own potatoes is buried treasure. They are harvested one or two at a time and make all the difference to a soup or stew.

So, at dusk on an autumn evening, I go out to the garden with a basket to see what might be for dinner. Groping under brown oak leaves, I find just enough young green spinach to thin out a few handfuls. Then I pull out little white turnips with their leaves and three leeks, snip some sprigs of marjoram and parsley. There are four potatoes in the kitchen. I go back inside, cut everything up, and put it in a pot with water to simmer as darkness thickens outside the windows. Tonight we will eat garden soup, which will taste of where we are.

Chapter 10 *Herbs*

Watching the medicinal trees shrubs and herbs in this way:
seeing their properties by their forms and colors and odors, and
their changes in character with the changes of the seasons, and
alternations of drought and plenty—how great is the wonder of
Nature! We note how substances are being elaborated into plants,
which we, wanting their help, know how to take at their crucial
moment: "now we must draw the resin, now we must take those
flowering tops."

Cameron Gruner, *The Canon of Medicine of Avicenna*

*S*ometimes I think about what I would do if my life
circumstances were to change radically—something I suppose
one should always expect—and instead of my long, rambling garden with a bit of nearly everything in it, I were to find myself with
only the tiniest yard, or perhaps just a balcony, on which to grow
things. Would I find a way to espalier a pear tree against a wall?
Grow rock plants in crevices? Which rose would I plant if I could
only have one? I am not sure. But I do know I would plant herbs,
at least a dozen different kinds. Once they grew, my garden would
be rich and strange, a world in miniature, full of interest and a
kind of rare companionship.

Herbs are the most individualized of plants. Each has something unmistakably distinctive about the form of flower or leaf:
gray-leaved lavender shrubs with purple flower spikes; thick,

ungainly leaves and stems of borage sending out fine-cut star flowers of intense cerulean blue; star-whorled vernal green leaves and minute white blossoms of woodruff. Herb scents are archetypal. Whoever sniffs chamomile, yarrow, *Melissa,* for the first time feels they have smelled them before. Perhaps this is ancestral memory of long-forgotten household remedies or spells, or perhaps it is that each separate scent corresponds with a particular state of soul.

Of all the plants in the garden, herbs have the longest and most pervasive relationship with human existence. Long ago all plants were called herbs. To leaf through a sixteenth-century English herbal, whose entries in turn refer back to sources in ancient Greece and Egypt, is to catch glimpses of a time in which the whole plant kingdom was seen as intertwined with human experience. Much of this connectedness has been forgotten, or dismissed since the Enlightenment and the dawn of modern science as primitive nature magic. The few hundred plants still called herbs—still prized as medicines, or seasonings, or alterers of mood—are survivors of a purge, not of the plants themselves but of our consciousness of them. Chamomile, foxglove, and parsley are still in cultivation because the lines from priests to apothecaries, monastery to Shaker village, Old Wife to housewife, and always gardener to gardener, remained unbroken. Information was transmitted along with tiny cuttings or roots, in little pots, from hand to hand, garden to garden.

Unlike other domestic plants—apples and pears, roses and carrots—the herbs have been largely unaltered by plant breeding over the millennia. Perhaps it was understood that their powers were too complex to isolate and refine, but stemmed from the totality of their plant being, their virtue living in their wildness. So the sage plant in a medieval woodcut, or the chamomile on an Egyptian sculpted relief, will look just the same as the ones basking in the sun near one's own kitchen door. Growing these deeply familiar, potent little plants, gardeners might begin to reconstruct a lost intimacy with the plant world or even create a new one.

Kitchen herbs

Most gardeners become acquainted with herbs when they grow a few for cooking. Dry herbs in packets are feeble ghosts of fresh ones, so any gardener who also cooks will want to plant an essential half dozen. Gardeners who do not have time or space to grow vegetables can grow herbs and still bring the tastes and smells of the garden to their meals.

Many gardeners who cook like to have on hand the constituents of the bouquet garni, the little bunch of herbs that French cooks tie together and drop into soups and stews. It is made of two or three sprigs of thyme, one of marjoram or oregano, some parsley, a bay leaf. Each of these herbs also has its own separate uses—marjoram goes well with green beans, thyme with chicken and fish. Also popular are a sage plant or two for meat, stuffings, baked squash, and dried beans, rosemary for marinades, or to snip onto lamb or onto roast potatoes and onions. All these plants are perennials that grow into nice woody bushes, although rosemary, marjoram, and bay are tender and must be put in pots and brought inside in winter wherever there is frost.

The fines herbes—dill, chervil, parsley, and tarragon—are often used all together in omelettes or sauces, but they also have their singular purposes: dill with cucumbers or salmon, chervil in soups, tarragon on chicken and deviled eggs, parsley on almost everything. Unlike the bouquet garni herbs, the delicate leaves of all the fines herbes are best if added fresh to a finished, or almost finished, dish, since their flavors are lost or changed in cooking. Chervil and dill are annuals that quickly go to seed and need several sowings a season for fresh supplies. Parsley is biennial, so it will survive the winter and come back green in early spring. Tarragon is perennial and sometimes difficult to find: it must be the "French" tarragon, *Artemisia dracunculus*. "Russian" tarragon is actually another plant altogether, with no taste.

Of course bouquets garnis and fines herbes derive from French cuisine, and recipes with sources in other cultures depend on different flavors altogether. Gardeners who cook in the Italian manner will want to grow fennel and basil. Mexican dishes need cilantro; Scandinavian ones, dill. I often wonder why particular cultures are drawn to such particular tastes. (It is not a simple matter of using what is locally available, as the long spice routes attest: Swedish Christmas cookies are flavored with Indian cardamom and English ones with ginger from Caribbean islands because those were the flavors those nations craved.) What might be learned about the nature of the culture or of the plant from a study of such affinities?

The herbs we know as kitchen herbs have even longer histories as medicine. In traditional cooking the functions of herbs as enhancers of flavor and as remedies are intertwined. Dill leaves snipped over cucumber, and caraway seeds in the cabbage, not only complement the flavor of these vegetables but dissipate the painful stomach gases they can otherwise stir up. The aromatic oils of sage and rosemary not only alleviate the sometimes gloomy weight of fatty meats and heavy starches, they also stimulate the digestion to work harder and cope with them. These are just crude examples of the refinements and transformation that herbs have brought to everyday cooking in the hands of knowing cooks all around the world.

Cook-gardeners have the great advantage that instead of going shopping to find particular herbs for a recipe, they can begin with what they have. They make experiments and explore, basing their exploration on a deepening acquaintance with the plants they grow. Cutting, tending, and propagating herbs, gardeners discover nuances in leaves, flowers, roots, and even in themselves.

Portrait of three herbs

Rosemary was the plant that invited me into the herb world. Because it will not survive temperatures below 25 degrees, I dug up my one small rosemary plant after its first summer in the garden and put it first into a pot on the doorstep and then, when it seemed settled in the pot, brought it into the house. There I got to know it better. Unlike many herbs rosemary thrives indoors in winter, especially if the house is as cold and damp as mine is. My rosemary grew nearly a foot that first winter; buds and new green shoots sprang from its woody stems. Several times it covered itself with a mist of pale blue flowers (the "dew of the sea" for which it is named). And it sent out a fragrance, which, I began to notice, could awaken my attention, bring me back to myself and my surroundings, encourage me when I needed encouragement.

Curious about this lovely and sympathetic plant, I consulted *A*

Modern Herbal by Maud Grieve, originally published in 1931 and reprinted since 1971 by Dover Press. Herbals have a fascination of their own. Some of the first written works were herbals: accounts of all that was known of the growing habits, friendly and unfriendly properties and uses of each plant, and their affinities with the planets and constellations. Different as they are from standard horticultural encyclopedias, there is something about these ostensibly unscientific works—which unapologetically mix practical instructions with cosmic connections, depiction of the outer world with that of inner sensibility—that makes a gardener feel instantly at home. Perhaps this is because gardeners themselves work with the same perceptual blend. Maud Grieve's is the most recent attempt at a serious, definitive "herbal" (she takes *herb* in its widest sense and one finds here histories of the daffodil and the onion as well as of angelica and boneset), and the author combines accurate botanical description, hints on cultivation, preparation, and uses (much of it based on her own rich experience), with a careful synopsis of references throughout the ages. I would recommend its two volumes to any gardener as a definite enhancer of the garden experience.

It was in *A Modern Herbal* that I found that the relationship of rosemary to awakening was not just my subjective discovery but a phenomenon that has been recognized for a long time. The *Grete Herbal,* first printed in England in 1530, prescribed rosemary for "weyknesse of ye brayne. Against weyknesse of the brayne and coldnesse thereof seythe rosemaria in wyne and let the patient receye the smoke at his nose and keep his heed warm." The martyr Sir Thomas More also loved rosemary for another kind of awakening, that of memory and faithfulness: "As for Rosmarine, I lette it runne all over my garden walls, not onlie because my bees love it but because it is the herb sacred to rememberence and therefore to friendship." When my doctor prescribed brushing my legs with rosemary oil (in the morning, but not at night in case it keep me from sleeping) to alleviate sluggish circulation, I was delighted, sure it would be just the thing, and it was. Perhaps I was drawn to rosemary because I particularly needed to wake up "heart, brayne and blood." The rosemary plants I brought in every year and replanted each spring eventually got too big and heavy to carry, so I made new plants from layerings and now have rosemaries gracefully leaning this way and that in many corners of the garden.

The resonance of rue is quite different from that of rosemary, as bitter and dark as rosemary is dewy and bright. Someone gave me a seedling once, and because I had read that it made a good companion for roses I planted it next to pink Queen Elizabeth. There the rue grew to about two feet, a billowing cloud of small, intricately lobed, blue-green leaves. It blossomed into small yellow flowers and dropped many seeds, which quickly made new plants that were easy to transplant. Rue is quite hardy, so it stays outside in winter, but I found that it needs a hard pruning as it begins to leaf out in spring, or it will become leggy and ragged, actually quite ugly. Cut back and allowed to make new wood each year, it has a stately beauty that belies its size.

The smell of rue is often called unpleasant, but I find its uncompromising bitterness compelling. There is no doubt that its oil and emanations are powerful; it is not a plant to handle lightly. I have read that merely touching rue brings out a rash in certain people, but this has not happened to anyone I know. Proximity to rue nearly killed an old bay laurel I had, which recovered as soon as I moved the plants apart, although the Queen Elizabeth rose has done very well with the rue right under it. Someone told me (but I have never tried this) that the oily exhalations of rue are so strong that if a match is lit a few inches above a plant on a hot sunny day, the air will ignite in a small explosion.

A sprinkling of finely chopped sweet basil and bitter rue is an incomparable enhancer of the flavor of plain broiled fish—flounder, bluefish, or cod. And one day an extremely old Italian woman came to a yard sale we had. She was not at all interested in what was for sale, but was excited about the rue plants she saw growing and told me (through her son, who interpreted) to pick sprigs of it in summer and store them in a jar with olive oil: in case of migraine they should be held to the forehead. I have tried this; while it does not stop the headache, its penetrating aroma creates islands of clarity and relief.

Other names for rue are herb of grace and herb of repentance. Grieve says this was because "holy water was sprinkled from brushes made of Rue at the ceremony usually preceding the Sunday celebration of High Mass." But I want to know *why* those brushes were made of rue. Was mad Ophelia's gift to her faithless and immobilized lover—"There's rue for you and here's some for me"—the energizing bitterness of penitence?

In its own sunny way chamomile is as powerful as mysterious rue. Where rue is bitter, chamomile is sweet; rue is dark, chamomile light. Chamomile is an annual, but readily seeds itself. Once one learns to recognize the minute cross-shaped seed leaves that reappear every spring, a permanent supply is ensured. To get the first lot started, the microscopic seeds need to be sown after the last frost or in early fall, and left uncovered. When it flowers, chamomile is a plant that warms the heart; its clouds of misty leaves and golden-centered white-petaled flowers are so pretty here and there in the flower beds or edging a bed of leeks, and its sweet, light scent fills the air when one works near it. It would be a joy to grow, even if it had no other qualities, but of course it does.

One would have to grow a lot of chamomile plants to harvest a supply of the famous tea, but a lot is not necessary to get the benefit of its medicinal effect. One teaspoon every hour of the infusion of a *single* chamomile flower, freshly picked if possible, in boiled water is an effective remedy for the kind of stomach flu in which a person cannot keep food or water down. Children usually like the taste and enjoy watching the preparation of a single flower especially for them. I can personally attest that it works just as well for adults. Besides soothing the stomach and intestines, chamomile calms nerves and works well against toothache, worries, and nightmares. Grieve cites the sixteenth-century herbalist Turner: "Thys herbe was coonsecrated by the Wyse men of Egypt unto the Sonne."

Cultivating herbs

As one might expect of plants that have survived intact for thousands of years, herbs are not difficult to grow. Many of the most familiar herbs originated around the shores of the Mediterranean and will grow best in conditions that approximate those of that region: plenty of sunshine and light, rocky soil. Small brittle leaves, such as those of thyme and savory, or needlelike ones, like rosemary or hyssop, and the silvery gray and fuzzy foliage of lavender and sage are all survival characteristics suitable for coping with long summer droughts.

The pioneering quality of herbs is what gives them their special characteristics. They are challenged by adversity. If herbs are overfertilized and make lush growth they often lose the pronounced shapes and scents that define them. The ideal soil for the Mediterranean herbs is a light, sandy one with a compost made mostly of plants. They are good plants to grow where water is scarce and the ground stony. Most of them love to cool their roots beneath a rock. Gardeners with heavy soils should work in a lot of leaf mold and other light composts, or create a small raised bed just for the herbs, double-dug and with plenty of compost incorporated into it. Raising the bed is for the sake of drainage; Mediterranean herbs will not survive standing water. Otherwise it is difficult to harm them.

Most Mediterranean herbs enjoy the sun, but many of the perennials can manage quite well in semishade; rosemary, in fact, seems to prefer it, and sage and lavender tolerate a little shade quite well. The annuals naturally want more of everything. Basil, chervil, and dill need full sun, and a richer soil, more compost. Parsley, as a biennial, falls somewhere in between; it takes its time and does not mind some shade.

Gardeners with little sun or heavy soil will do better with the herbs that originated on forest floors or beside shady streams. Many powerful native American herbs are shade-loving plants of the forest: wild ginger, ginseng, goldenseal. Bee balm will tolerate some shade and likes a rich soil; its leaves make a sweet tea and its flamelike scarlet flowers draw hummingbirds. Woodruff actually thrives in shade and makes a lovely ground cover. With its pretty green leaf whorls and tiny white flowers that open in May, it grows where nothing else seems to. The mints grow anywhere at all, but need a bed to themselves because their underground runners go so fast.

Planting herbs

Many useful annual herbs are so short-lived that it is hardly worth growing them except by direct seeding. Dill, which is very hardy, still needs to be planted every three or four weeks if one really wants a serious supply of fresh green leaves. The same is true of basil, which also needs serial plantings to keep it sweet, although pinching off the flowers helps prolong it. I have noticed, however, that the lovely globe basil, which grows into a pretty miniature bush about four inches tall with leaves the size of mouse ears, keeps its delicate flavor all season. A few of these little plants (bought as plants or seeded) might be enough to put in salads and add to the cooking. But if one wants fresh pesto all summer, then two or three sowings of plain, Genoa basil are what is needed.

Parsley, a biennial, is famous for being slow to germinate. The story goes that it needs to go down to the devil seven times before it can germinate. The secret of growing parsley is not to give up too soon and then, when it does come up, to leave it where it is, as it does not transplant well.

Most of the perennial herbs are quite difficult to grow from seed. Lavender, thyme, and rosemary need a good place indoors, skill, and vigilance. The seeds are minuscule and difficult to handle, and when they finally germinate they grow so slowly that it is a long time before one can plant them outside without fear of losing them. There are exceptions; rue, for instance, and sage germinate readily even outdoors. At the opposite extreme is French tarragon that for some peculiar reason does not come true from seed at all.

Luckily there are plenty of other ways to come by perennial herb plants. One of the best sources is other people's gardens. Different people develop sympathies with different herbs and when they do, they tend to grow a lot of them. My healthiest sage plants are eighteen years old and four feet tall and come from the garden of a friend who loves sage so much he grew a whole hedge of it—a lovely sight when it was in bloom with its pink-mauve flowers in May, all silvery-green leaves and hoary stems the rest of the year. Since becoming a rosemary enthusiast, I have got into the habit of making layerings from my plants whenever I see a low-lying branch (see chapter 5). I pot them up at the end of summer and have more plants than I have room for in the fall, so I give them away. Rosemary, as Thomas More remarked, is a good way to be remembered.

Even if a gardener has no extra plants to spare, he or she can almost always spare a cutting. Most herbs propagate easily from stems or leaves (see chapter 5). And the best way to get French tarragon is to confidently advise a friend who has one that his or her plant is much too big and needs dividing at the root.

Garden centers carry a bigger selection of herbs than they used to, the "medicinals" as well as the culinary ones. But any gardener who has a chance to visit an herb nursery should seize the opportunity. Herb nurseries are usually run by enthusiasts. No one else would bother with raising St. John's Wort, mountain arnica, or wild persimmon trees for the sake of the two or three customers a year who might want them, or perhaps simply for the sake of the plants themselves.

To wander through a field of lavender and step into a small greenhouse in which three or four hundred different kinds of plants are cheerfully putting out new leaves—each with a history of human association that is thousands of years old, each with a highly idiosyncratic shape, smell, and being—is like entering a temple of gardening. There are two such herb farms within a day's journey from where I live: one, the Peconic River Herb Farm among cranberry bogs on the shores of Long Island's only river, the other, the venerable Meadowbrook Herb Garden, biodynamic for forty years, in a section of Rhode Island known for the diversity of its ferns and other native flora.

Many years ago a few miles from Meadowbrook I was surprised to see the familiar shape of a Long Island neighbor, the Native American herbalist Red Thunder Cloud, bent over, intent on picking plants by the side of the green Rhode Island back

road, as I often saw him engaged on the dunes and by the road-
sides at home. We stopped the car to say hello and asked him if he
too were bound for the herb farm. No, he said, he did not know
it, but Native Americans had historically traveled to that part of
Rhode Island in early summer for the sake of the rare medicinal
plants that grew there, and he came there every year. Since then I
have wondered if it is generally true of herb farms that they are
located in places of unusual natural vitality and if the plants cultivated there draw virtue from the nature of the places where they
are.

Medicine for the garden

I began this discussion of herbs by saying that a dozen or so by
themselves might be enough to bring a tiny garden to life. But I
should also mention the role that herbs play, in a garden of any
size, in creating small but powerful points of influence, helpful not
just to the gardener but to the other plants in the garden. Some
gardeners like to create herb gardens or beds within their larger
garden. This can be pretty and useful (especially keeping the
kitchen herbs together so nongardeners in the family can find
them). But one might also choose to disperse them here and there
for the sake of their beneficial effects on the garden as a whole.
Many plants that are medicine for the human body or soul are
also medicine for the garden, for its soil and air and the roots of
plants.

Comfrey is a plant whose delicate mauve flower bells look
lovely in the perennial bed (moreover, its leaves make effective
poultices for bruises, sprains, and even fractures). But its roots are

so invasive that I would not plant it in the flower bed if I did not also use it as a harvest for the compost heap. Comfrey is a most valuable compost ingredient, a rich source of potassium, phosphorus, and calcium. Every year when the comfrey has finished flowering, I pull out whole plants—leaves, roots, and all—enough to fill a wheelbarrow, which I then push down to my pile. There will still be plenty left for more flowers next spring.

Valerian and yarrow are two more herbs that look lovely in a flower bed. Valerian, also called garden heliotrope, has tall pale pink inflorescences growing out of light green spirals of leaves. It has a strange, musky smell, and its roots (which are a powerful sedative, too powerful for amateur herbalists to experiment with) are a magnet to earthworms.

Lacelike white yarrow flowers (the plain *Achillea millefolium,* not the varieties that are bred for color) make a tea that is useful in colds with fevers; it will raise the sweat that breaks the fever. Like valerian, yarrow is one of the six plants used in the biodynamic compost preparations, its role there having to do with making plants more receptive to certain trace elements. But it is not only helpful in the compost. Rudolf Steiner said of yarrow, "Like some sympathetic people in human society who exert an influence just by their presence and not by what they say, yarrow's mere presence in areas where it grows abundantly is extremely beneficial." The yarrow in my flower bed and on the edges of the vegetable garden is not planted, it just happens to show up and I leave it where it is.

Of chamomile—which is lovely wherever it grows between the lettuces, in among the perennials, here and there in a lawn— Grieve writes that "It has been called the 'Plant's Physician.' . . . It has been stated that nothing contributes so much to the health of a garden as a number of chamomile herbs dispersed about it, and that if another plant is drooping and sickly, in nine cases out of ten it will recover if you place a herb of chamomile near it." Chamomile is in the compost preparation that has to do with stabilizing nitrogen. It is also recommended as an excellent companion plant in the vegetable garden and as a crust-breaker for soil that is hardening and deficient in calcium and potassium. So one might as well grow it.

Not all the herbs that help the garden are so obviously congenial. Stinging nettle is a plant more often known as an odious weed than as an herb. It spreads quickly with underground runners, is not pretty, and does give a burning sting to bare skin. But there are gardeners, and I am one, who actually cultivate it, not in the flower bed it is true, but in a thick clump behind the compost heap.

Nettle is a highly concentrated source of iron. As an anemic person, I drink a tonic tea made from its young leaves, which come up in early spring, when I feel I need it most. The garden also drinks nettle tea, an incomparable foliar and soil food. The nettles are cut (with one's gloves on) before they have flowered and immersed in a barrel or bucket of water, then covered and left standing for about two weeks. After that interval the tea will smell terrible, so terrible that one will quickly be convinced of its seriousness. One strains off the liquid and sprays it over plants and soil (the smell quickly goes away once the tea is out of the bucket). The role of nettle in compost preparations is, as Rudolf Steiner wrote, "to make the soil more intelligent, so that it individualizes itself and conforms to the particular plants that you grow in it."

Several times I have made the experiment of grasping the nettle without gloves and it hurts much less than an accidental brush, which feels a bit like a burn. While their sting is neither lasting nor dangerous, it would probably not be a good idea to give nettles the run of the garden. But gardeners who venture further into Steiner's *Agriculture* will not despise them:

> Stinging nettle also carries the radiations and currents of potash and calcium, but in addition it has a kind of iron radiation that is nearly as beneficial for the whole of nature as the iron radiations in our blood are for us. Because it is such a good influence, the stinging nettle we find growing wild does not deserve our customary scorn. It should really be growing all around our hearts, since the role it plays in nature by virtue of its marvelous inner structure and way of working is very similar to that of the heart in the human organism.

Chapter 11 Trees in the Garden

It may be, then, that some little root of the sacred tree still lives.
Nourish it then that it may leaf and blossom and fill with singing
birds.

Black Elk

*P*eople plant trees when someone dies or is born
because trees, with their roots deep in the ground and their
branches lifted toward heaven, are a picture of life itself. In the
Norse myths Ygdrasil is a rowan tree with three roots: one in the
underworld, one in the kingdom of men, and one in the realm of
the gods. The Nydhog serpent gnaws at the root in the underworld, steadily undermining the whole creation; meanwhile up
in the branches four stags graze on leaves and drip magical dew
into the mouths of sleeping Lif and Lifthrasir, the man and woman
of the future. The first temples were sacred groves, and when,
later, Greeks sculpted their columns of marble, they still recalled
the trunks of trees, even as they also took on the proportions of
the human figures. A great forest resembles a Gothic cathedral, but
this is because those cathedrals were made to be like forests.

Taking care of trees is not the same as tending the green plants
that are born and die within a few short months or years. Old

trees tower overhead; perhaps they rustled in the wind long before their gardeners were born. New trees grow into an unimaginable future those gardeners may never see. Without trees a garden is flat, all on the ground. A treeless garden does not resonate. Trees give the garden its voice, murmuring in breezes, roaring in storms; their branches are choir stalls for birds. Trees connect earth and sky, frame distant views.

The garden gets its enclosure, its placeness, from trees. Yet a tree can be a garden's most serious limitation. It may radically restrict what can be grown there by casting too heavy a shadow, or mat the earth with invasive roots to the point where a gardener some-times must choose between the tree and the garden.

There is no simple resolution to the tension between a love for trees and a gardener's desire to grow many kinds of plants, or between a longing for shelter and shade and the realization that the tree planted today may not mature till the gardener has moved on to a different garden, or a different world. Contemplating planting or cutting down a large tree, gardeners must watch care-fully, then decide; then they wait and watch the results of the deci-sion. Grappling with tree riddles, one grapples with time and change, the stuff of life itself.

Trees and time

Sometimes fate brings a gardener to the perfect moment in the lives of the trees and the life of the garden. This happened to a woman I know, who recently moved into a little house around the cove from mine. The house was run-down and had to be fixed. There was no garden as such, just a small meadow of poor soil, roughly mown grass, wildflowers, and weeds. But three perfect trees grew there, each in the perfect place.

At the center of the meadow and at the summit of its gentle slope, a spreading apple tree, thirty feet tall, blossoms sweetly in the spring and in summer casts a dappled green shade where people love to gather and sit. In the autumn, it delivers a crop of tart red apples with which to make pies. To the north a dark pine protects the house from winter winds. Twenty feet behind the house, shading its roof but not the garden, rises a tulip tree. Its straight trunk points its forty-foot length at the sky, while its black branches cascade downward, full of huge-petaled orange "tulip" blossoms in spring, pale gold leaves in autumn, in winter a frozen waterfall against the sky. It will take years to repair the house and improve the garden soil, but because of those trees my friend felt at home from the day she arrived.

Most of the time, destiny is not so kind. It brings challenges: not enough trees or too many, or trees of good size and place but dying. Time does not stand still in the garden. The friend who happened onto perfect trees is a gardener, so one of her first acts on taking possession of that place was to plant two young pear trees, each three feet tall. One day—in her lifetime or someone else's—the old apple tree will be gone and the pears ready to take its place.

Planting trees

If planting a seed is an act of faith and imagination, planting a tree, or sometimes taking one down, is even more so. The effects on the landscape will be defining, and will not really be seen for a long time. Among the first questions a gardener needs to ask are how big the tree will ultimately grow and how long it will take to get there.

It helps to be old enough to have watched a few trees grow. In London, there is a place where I can spy on the garden of the house in which I grew up. My mother planted a Scots pine there when I was seven; it was then a little taller than I was and more or less the pyramidal shape of a Christmas tree. Forty years later, it branches high off a gnarled trunk. At fifty feet tall, with long, swaying horizontal boughs, it fulfills its mission to hide the black bricks of the house opposite. It also softens the air and muffles the roar of city traffic with the sighing of its branches, thrush songs, and crooning pigeons. Our family has not lived in that house for many years, but though I have not met them, I see new children at play beneath my mother's pine.

My own children dug up a three-inch white pine seedling from a crowd of them in the woods and planted it in our present garden. That was ten years ago and now it is twenty feet tall. It is twelve years since friends planted a seven-foot tulip tree with a trunk two inches thick near their farmhouse door. It now has a thick trunk and reaches their high roof even though, as can happen, a hurricane blew the tree's top branches off four years after planting. The year-old seedling peach tree someone brought us in a flower pot made peaches of its own in four years.

Although only seeing is truly convincing, a good reference book is an invaluable tool for envisioning the future. Hugh Johnson's *International Book of Trees* not only has lively, informative text and extraordinary photographs of trees in both gardens and their native habitats, it also has enlightening comparative growth charts and a comprehensive tree index. There one learns, for example, that a silver maple can reach fifty feet in twenty years, whereas an American holly is likely to grow only eight feet in the same period. This kind of information is based on averages, and one must consider that a tree naturally grows faster under conditions where it feels at home and very much slower (if at all) in alien surroundings.

Especially if there is a need for shelter or protection, gardeners' natural inclination is often to look for trees that grow very quickly, or to plant the biggest trees they can afford. But these strategies do not always work. If the tree one loves and desires—perhaps it is a weeping willow—happens to be fast-growing, then this is all well and good. The willow will be huge and murmurous in ten years. But the tree that grows fast is not always the tree one wants.

It is in the nature of fast-growing trees to send out roots sideways and close to the surface of the soil, rather than roots that grow down deep and straight. This means that the roots will take up a lot of garden space, and also that the tree will always be vulnerable to sudden upending in storms with high winds and heavy rains. Sometimes one's heart's desire happens to be a tree that grows very slowly—a white oak, say, or a black mulberry. Surely one must plant it anyway, even if one may never see the tree in its maturity. Often a mixture of fast trees and slow will work best. A deodar cedar can be nurse tree to hollies. If the garden is very windy or is exposed to a road, a shelter-belt of fast trees, perhaps a row of poplars, will give protection and privacy while slower trees grow up.

Planting a tree already grown to large size is a serious affair. It is not something one can do on one's own, even with a friend or two to help. Trucks, tree spades, and guy wires enter the picture. A lot of money changes hands and there is always a considerable element of risk. It is true that these days expert crews can move huge trees that do survive. But even gardeners who can afford the expenditure and effort must consider seriously if this kind of sudden readjustment is what they want.

Trees take on much of their form and character from the place where they put down their roots—the soil and rocks, the water underground, the quality of light, and prevailing winds. A tree that has grown up in a particular landscape reveals something essential about the history and character of that place: the place changes the tree, and the tree changes the place. Perhaps I would be taken in by the stability of a venerable oak that was in fact slipped into place only yesterday, but I suspect some part of me would be made uneasy by the absence of a fundamental relatedness.

A young whip—so-called because that is what they look like, just a trunk, pliant, and so slender one can hardly see it—has little readjustment to make. It has, as yet, few roots to be disturbed, so it will be free to develop its own root system in the manner most appropriate to the place it is given. It goes easily into the ground, needing only a hole about two feet deep, some compost mixed with the soil, and a short stake, to which it is loosely tied for support. A little watering and keeping the weeds and grasses away from its roots are all the care it needs. A tree that is four or five years older does seem to offer more substance at first, but very often the whip, with its strong start and nothing to overcome, will quickly overtake it.

While a tree grows

Though starting small may be better for the tree, it may seem too bleak a beginning for a garden that feels empty and flat, nor will it seem able to fill the enormous void that always opens up where a great tree once stood. But ways can be found to plant young trees that will infuse the space with life from the very beginning.

A sapling all by itself looks, and sometimes really is, too lonely. Often what is wanted is not one tree but two or three that will grow up together, as individuals but also as a single conversing entity: a grove. Suddenly there is not just the trees but the space between them. Between young trees, or around a single one (sometimes there needs to be just one), shrubs and herbaceous plants that have associations with the tree can be planted, so that one is planting not just a tree but a whole plant community.

Often the best examples of what such a grouping might consist of are found in the wild places not far from one's own garden. In the woods closest to my house, high-bush blueberry, sweet fern, and American holly grow in among the oaks, and fragrant native azaleas flower under red maples; in the moors near the ocean bright red winterberries begin to gleam just as the shad trees drop their last golden leaves. In making a tree place, rather than a solitary tree, one creates what very quickly becomes a vivid presence in the garden, full of flowers and singing birds. And the trees themselves draw nourishment and shelter from the company of congenial plants and grow stronger and faster.

Also following the example of the forest, a tree surgeon I know often encourages his clients to leave the trunk standing when a big tree dies in place, at least while the young tree (or trees) planted to replace it is still small. He saws off the branches to prevent them from falling, but finds that even a dead trunk shelters young saplings and that its gradual decomposition nourishes them. Dead trees also give homes to birds, especially woodpeckers, and to butterflies. Not everyone wants a dead tree trunk in their garden, of course, and if the tree has died of a disease or a hostile beetle it needs to be quickly taken away. So leaving such relics will not always work. But in the gardens I visit where the ruin of an old tree (sometimes with vines or climbing roses trained on it) has been left to stand beside tender saplings, I do not see desolation but continuity and unexpected beauty.

A last consideration, but perhaps most important, is that while it may be possible to predict the number of inches or feet a tree will grow each year, a young tree's effect on the gardener is much less calculable. A callow sapling that can barely support a perching bird often occupies a disproportionately large space in a gardener's attention. Watching as buds become branches, which in turn yield more buds and more branches, seeing up close the unfurling of leaves, their shapes, the first subtle flowerings of forest trees—all this can so absorb a gardener that he or she loses interest in how long it will be till the branches hide the house next door. Then, quite suddenly, they do.

Big trees

In *The Education of a Gardener,* the great landscape designer Russell Page wrote about the difficulties presented by big forest trees in small gardens:

> When they are already there or for some reason you want to plant them, you must, I think make them the main feature of the garden and then design or plant around them. You must work with them and never against them. It is useless to fight a battle you can only lose in trying to grow roses or delphiniums or annuals anywhere near a big tree.

This is true enough, but gardeners react to this situation in various ways. Some gardeners, especially if they have exceptional trees (I am thinking of a garden near here devoted entirely to three magnificent beeches), reconcile themselves to whatever shade-loving understory planting they can manage, even if, as with the beeches, it is hardly any. Other gardeners, myself among

them, fight the losing battle anyway, getting branches cut out here and there to let in more light, and stubbornly persisting with roses, delphiniums, lettuces. To some extent one can compensate for a lack of sunlight by enriching the soil, with more manure, more compost. But only up to a point. There comes a moment when it is clear a choice must be made and gardeners begin to contemplate cutting down the tree.

Powerful emotion always surrounds the felling of big trees, and this is especially true now, when so many people are haunted by the specter of environmental decline. This year when a northeaster tore through our village, taking its usual toll of three or four maples and a willow or two, the chief of the highway department shocked many by telling a newspaper reporter that he "did not see what all the fuss was about." Trees always fall down in storms, new trees come up, he said, noting that the Village Tree Committee had planted twelve new street trees that very fall. Such is life. He is right, of course, but I think the extra note of "fuss" he heard above the roar of the chain saws stemmed from the sense of millennial crisis, of a planet running down, that adds foreboding to regret with the crash of each falling tree. Gardeners, though they may share this feeling, have their mandate to keep planting, which helps them remain not unmoved, but calmer and able to make necessary discriminations.

Some trees really are more worth saving than others. Gardeners must consider each tree's individual history and future, its compatibility, or lack of it, with other plants. Perhaps the tree in the way is a nobly formed sixty-foot white oak that has taken a hundred years to reach its size and shape, and might live another century. A thoughtful gardener might very well make the decision to keep it and look for ways, as Page suggests, to make the tree itself the garden's focus.

Oaks have high canopies and they leaf out slowly in the springtime. Therefore many plants will grow happily beneath them, bushes and lovely woodland flowers, even small trees. The choice of plants may be restricted, but the garden can still be beautiful if the gardener decides to accept the limitation. Then, having made a conscious decision to keep a tree, one might become inspired to take care of it. A gardener might check to make sure the tree's roots are not being compacted by cars driving over them. An understory planting of bushes and flowers, whose dropping leaves can be left to decompose, will nourish an established tree; a raked lawn will not (and "lawn-care" in the form of weed killers is a gradual but sure way to kill big, shallow-rooted trees such as beeches).

Pruning of high branches has to be done by a person who has the training and equipment to safely climb a tree with a heavy saw, and who also has the sensitivity and understanding to know where and how to cut. Hiring a good tree surgeon is an expense, but usually the job only needs to be done every decade or so, and with such care the tree will live longer and be more beautiful. It is primarily a matter of cutting out dead or damaged branches and those with steep crotches, which collect rainwater and harbor rot.

There are, however, many situations where it would be better for the garden, and even the planet, to simply take a tree out. When a big tree falls or is cut down, a huge expanse of sky appears and a sudden surge of energy explodes on the ground. Where one tree stood, a dozen bushes with flowers and berries, a vegetable garden, roses, and two or three small trees could flourish. Perhaps from this diversity more will be gained for the future than is lost.

Where I live, the tree in the way of the morning sun is almost invariably a Norway maple. Norway maples were introduced to the United States in this century and are now showing signs of taking over our entire village, which was once as diverse as an arboretum. They are as vigorous as weeds, will easily grow thirty-five feet in twenty years, and do so as soon as one's back is turned. At full size, they cast shadows so deep that only more Norway maples will grow beneath them. I have felt no qualms at all about cutting down several maple saplings on the edges of my garden.

The ideal is to find places for forest trees so that even when they reach full height they will not come between the rest of the garden and the sun. Gardens thrive in an open southern exposure, with which the plants will receive sunlight in the morning, while they still have dew on them. If deciduous trees stand to the west, their shadows will fall in the afternoon, when many plants and most gardeners will enjoy them. Often the best place for a tall forest tree is as a "dooryard tree," within twenty or thirty feet of the house, ideally to the southwest so it will cool the roof in summer.

A dooryard tree can be a kind of presiding spirit for a household, marking the door and happily modifying the life within. Our house has such a tree—a Norway maple, but beloved anyway. The roof rises up into its branches so in summer one cannot quite tell roof from leafy canopy, and the tree leans gently toward the house. When I wake on breezy spring mornings to sunlight filtered through waving green leaves at the window, I feel as though I am in a nest. My daughter sits up on her bed and laughs at the squirrels. In winter we watch the stars through the frame of its bare branches. That maple is dying now; I should have cut it down and replaced it long ago, but I did not have the heart, so now I must. If we choose and plant its successor well, we can watch its steady climb into the future.

Small trees

> Without such trees one cannot create a hermitage,
> but where there are trees it is easy.
>
> *Yuan Yeh*

If big forest trees can be difficult to integrate in gardens, though worth the effort, small trees seem to be made for them. These are understory trees, which grow no taller than twenty-five feet at maturity—hollies, shadbush, dogwoods, hawthorns, magnolias, yews, and many fruit trees: crabapples and quinces, peaches and plums or the semidwarf apples, pears, and cherries. These trees can mark the end of one part of the garden or the beginning of

another, make a grove to sit in, or just stand beautifully by themselves. Two or three trees whose forms are strongly horizontal,
dogwoods, for instance, or snowbells, which have branches that
grow out sideways almost as far as their trunks are high, can give a
part of the garden a roof of floating green leaves and white bracts,
as their long branches reach out to one another. In summer one
might set a table and chairs under the green roof and turn part of
the garden into an airy house.

A garden orchard

Perhaps because of school scripture lessons, the very word *garden*
summons to my mind the image of an apple tree in bloom,
although sometimes I see a pear. Fruit trees have grown in gardens
since gardening began. Their spurred branches against pale spring
skies or fruiting near a wall resonate as though one had seen them
over and again through many lifetimes. The gardener takes care of
the tree and the tree takes care of the gardener with flowers, green
shade, and sweet fruit.

It is probably mythologically appropriate that these most allur-
ing of trees should be difficult to grow. Gardeners need to think
over their side of the bargain very carefully before actually going
out to plant one. Unlike the herbs, brought into gardens straight
out of nature, the plump shapes and sweet taste of apples and pears
are the work of inspired graftings and crossbreedings of Persian
gardeners thousands of years ago, their varieties continuously
modified ever since. Being so much shaped for human ends,
orchard trees, like sheep or cows, demand human care. Care of
fruit trees is not so very time-consuming, far fewer minutes per

year than tending a perennial border or vegetable bed, but they do take attention. Fruit trees ask for vigilance, they demand that their gardeners become intimate with local conditions of soil and weather, and with the trees' cycles of growth. They need gardeners to stay alert, ready to do the right thing at the right moment. Since learning these things is one reason people are drawn to their gardens, gardeners sometimes discover that taking care of fruit trees is not so much a burden as an intensification of what they already love.

CHOOSING VARIETIES

The main reason that fruit trees can be difficult is their susceptibility to insect pests and disease. It seems counter to the spirit of contemplative gardening to struggle for one's plants, and, certainly, to poison them. So if growing fruit trees has to mean fighting a long battle against fire blight, scab, and apple maggots, one might decide against it. But most gardeners, if they think about it, have seen at least one old apple or pear tree that thrives year after year with little care or none at all. Such a tree is invariably the right tree in the right place. If a gardener can establish this happy situation from the beginning, then the continuing relationship is likely to be a harmonious one. Planting the right tree is therefore the first, often the most important, part of fruit tree care.

A tree that will be full of problems and disease in one place will be healthy and fruitful in another. This is why hundreds of varieties of apples and dozens of pears have been developed and treasured over the millennia. The very local science of what fruit tree to plant where almost became lost knowledge in this century because of two related phenomena. Mass marketing forced orchardists to grow the same few varieties (bushels after bushels of Red Delicious apples and Bartlett pears) no matter where they lived. The development of chemical insecticides and fungicides allowed them to do it. Today, few farmers know the names of the varieties their forebears depended on, and few tree nurseries grow them.

Once again, almost-lost knowledge has continued to be cultivated in gardens. Where an orchardist might have pulled out the Newtown Pippins or Northern Spies, gardeners often retained them. If one has the luck, the very best way to find the right tree for one's garden is if a neighbor in a similar situation has a thriving tree and still knows what it is called. One may well be able to track it down through one of the nurseries that specialize in old varieties. Ordering fruit trees by mail is perfectly all right because by far the best planting practice is to start with dormant year-old trees, and these bear shipping well.

Sometimes one discovers a variety recurring throughout a region, bearing beautifully and resisting all diseases, but with no known name. It may in fact never have had one. In such a case a really adventurous gardener can ask for some scion wood—cuttings a few inches long—to graft into new little trees. There are nurseries that will do this to order by mail, grafting the scions one sends—one must consult carefully about timing—to the rootstock of one's choice (see Readings and Resources section at the end of the book for addresses of fruit nurseries and grafters).

Besides researching old knowledge, gardeners can take advantage of the new. As disenchantment with pesticides grows, nurseries and agricultural agents are able to recommend more and more new fruit-tree varieties that have been developed for resistance to particular pests and disease. This may sound a rather dull and unromantic way to choose a fruit tree, but it is not. A scabby apple is not romantic, even if it grows on a tree called Maiden's Blush. In my garden the new, scab-resistant Liberty bears the loveliest apple blossoms I have ever seen, large pale pink drooping petals, and its apples taste like sweet wine. It is heartening to know that not all garden wisdom grows out of the past.

ROOTSTOCKS

All apple and pear trees are grafted, and the rootstocks on which they grow also influence a tree's ability to thrive in particular climates and soils. Most fruit nurseries offer each variety on a choice of several rootstocks. So gardeners do need to research local recommendations for rootstocks as well as for varieties.

The rootstock is also what determines the ultimate size of the tree. In recent decades there has been a bias toward very small fruit trees, the dwarfs, which means anything from ten feet down to the size of an average tomato plant. The reasoning for this is that these treelings bear fruit quickly—as early as their second year—are easy to pick from, and fit into small spaces. This will tempt some gardeners. But gardeners should also consider that fruit trees are usually healthier and certainly hardier on roots that allow them to grow bigger. Besides this practical consideration, and, especially since this chapter is really more about growing trees than growing fruit, I will go so far as to recommend that gardeners grow the biggest size trees that will fit on their site.

It is true that a semidwarf apple, for example, growing on a good all-purpose rootstock (like MM111), will not bear much fruit for four or five years. But it will reach fifteen or twenty feet, have branches sturdy enough to climb into, green shade in summer, and a fountain of blossom in spring. It will still be the soul of the garden many years after the dwarfs have given up the ghost (dwarfs seldom live much past twenty years) and will give structure and history to the garden. I have always wished I had room for a standard apple tree, which, although they take between five and ten years to bear fruit, often grow to thirty or forty feet, live a hundred years, and can feed several families. Such trees are landmarks, and getting scarce—what a tree to plant to celebrate a newborn child.

SITING THE TREES

The right place for a fruit tree is in full sunlight. Apples can tolerate a very little shade, but pears, peaches, and plums cannot. Then, there must be enough room for the trees to grow into their proper shapes. An orchard of two graceful, spreading trees will be lovelier and more rewarding than a cramped cluster of six or seven. (One well-grown apple or pear tree can have as much character as a whole orchard, but there must be other apple or pear trees growing in nearby gardens or the fruit will not be pollinated.) Fruit trees need to be planted well away from the roots of other trees, and usually will need as much space from one another as the height they will ultimately reach. For example, semidwarf apples or pears should be spaced at least fifteen feet from trunk to trunk.

Another essential factor is placing the trees in the right flow of air. If rough winds blow through an orchard when it blooms, bees cannot pollinate the trees. On the other hand, if light breezes cannot penetrate, then leaves stay damp too long after wet or humid weather, which leads to fungus infections. What is needed are tree places that are sheltered without being stagnant.

PLANTING

Orchard soil need not be rich, but the spot where each tree will be planted should be well prepared and kept free of weeds. Whenever it is possible, it is a good idea to prepare the tree holes in the autumn before spring planting, so as to be able to put the trees in the ground as early as possible in spring. When this is not possible, one waits for the soil to properly thaw and then dry out and hopes that any trees ordered by mail do not arrive too soon (a good reason to order from nurseries to the north of where one lives).

In any case, the hole must be dug about two feet deep (deeper, if one hits hardpan). In doing this one separates the topsoil, which will go back in the hole, from the subsoil that one wheelbarrows away to the compost heap. When the topsoil goes back in, it is time to incorporate a couple of wheelbarrows of well-aged manure or good garden compost.

To give a tree the best start, it should be planted at one year old, when it will be about four feet tall, with buds but no branches. If it has come through the mail and one cannot plant it right away, it is best to heel it into the soil or compost heap, making sure the roots and lower trunk are completely covered, or if this isn't possible, to store it in the coolest place one can find that does not freeze. As soon as the ground has begun to warm up, the little tree should go into its predug hole. Before the tree is planted, its roots should be soaked in a bucket of water for a few hours. While it is thus awakening, one prepares the hole, makes a little mound of soil on which to seat the tree, then hammers in a stout stake a good two feet into the ground two or three inches from where the trunk will stand (the stake will stay till the tree is four or five years old).

One then takes up the tree, gently spreads its roots apart and settles it into its hole, distributing the roots so that they fall about the little center mound and making sure that the graft mark will be a few inches above level ground. (If the graft is buried the tree will grow into a standard!) It is nice to have someone hold the tree upright while one refills the hole with compost and topsoil, but I have also managed by holding the trunk with one hand and throwing in the soil with the other. In either case, one must work carefully, making sure the roots are well covered, with no trapped air spaces. Then one spades on more compost and topsoil till the ground is level, tamps it down with firm footsteps, ties the trunk to the stake and gently soaks it down, stands back, and makes a wish.

CULTIVATION

Until the tree is fully grown, it is important not to let grass grow around its trunk, as this will rob its roots of moisture and nourishment. Each tree needs to stand in its own cultivated place, a circle of earth extending around about four or five feet from its trunk. This should be kept clear of old leaves and twigs (which can harbor disease and nesting pests) and livened up with shallow hoeings now and again. Early in spring and late in autumn one feeds the trees by shoveling on more composted manure, leaving a little space open just around the trunk. The soil under the tree need not stay bare. Spring bulbs and summer annuals do not get in the way of cultivation, and daffodils in spring, cornflowers and nasturtiums (supposed to deter aphids) in summer, look pretty under young green limbs.

TRAINING AND PRUNING OF YOUNG TREES

The training and pruning of very young trees only takes a few minutes, since there is so little to train and prune. But these few minutes will determine the shape of the future tree. Few small moves in gardening have such powerful effects.

In order to establish a central leader form (see chapter 7), pruning the first year involves one cut (as soon as the tree is planted) in which one looks for a healthy bud a foot or so down from the top of the trunk and cuts just above it. This bud will become the leader, the vertical central point of the tree (if it gets damaged, as can happen, one can begin again the next year, choosing another bud). The following year one chooses the three or four branches that will become the tree's framework: the main, horizontal fruit-bearing branches of the tree. These framework branches should begin at least two feet off the ground and point out in four different directions. Once they are chosen, one favors them, ensuring they will not be overshadowed by removing competing branches and buds (but still taking care to save enough leafy branches to keep the tree healthy and for spares).

To be fruitful, branches must be somewhat horizontal: an angle of thirty degrees between branch and trunk is the ideal. Branches only rarely grow this way without guidance. An effective way to help is to attach an ordinary clothespin in the crotch between a newly developing branch bud and the trunk of the tree. The branch has to grow out past the clothespin and this already gives it a better angle. Later on, but when the branches are still young and pliable, one can gently pull them down by using string attached to pegs in the ground. This is done as the branches leaf out in spring, and the strings are untied in summer so the branches do not snap in storms.*

PROTECTION

In winter, rabbits and deer love to eat fruit-tree bark, and this is often the end of young trees. Wrapping the little trunks in hardware cloth will prevent this. In springtime, or whenever there are enough green plants that the rabbits and deer will have found something else to eat, the trees should be unwrapped lest mice or other pests make nests around the trunk.

GROWING FOR FRUIT

In three or four years, if the tree is a semidwarf apple, or in two or three, if it is a peach or plum, the tree will begin to bear. The first crop will only be a scattering, but still a triumphant moment in the life of the garden. Who gets to pick the first apple? Who cuts it open? Who eats it?

Many gardeners will be perfectly happy just to take what comes in the way of fruit. Some years there will be baskets of

---

*The foregoing is a broad sketch of one way to train a young tree that works well for apples and pears, also plums and peaches. To learn about other methods readers should look at specialized books on pruning. *The Complete Guide to Pruning and Training Plants,* by David Joyce and Christopher Brickell, is excellent. Also, proper timing is important in pruning fruit trees and varies with each climate: it is therefore sensible at first to check with the agricultural extension service in your area for local recommendations.

wormy apples for pies, or peaches for jam. Other years the fruit may be perfect; if one has been very lucky with the variety and weather, this will happen quite often; if not so lucky, the tree will still be lovely, and unscarred fruit an occasional happy surprise.

Other gardeners will want to move toward reliable bushels of homegrown fruit, to serious fruit-growing rather than simply care of the tree and taking what comes. Taking the steps above will be the best possible beginning: choosing the right variety, finding a good planting spot and digging a good hole, hoeing and composting, pruning and training. If the tree is healthy and strong it will have the best chance of fighting off disease and surviving pest incursions—the two major causes of crop failures. Keeping the tree areas clean and cultivated is also a vital step in avoiding some of the worst orchard pests: apple maggot and plum curculio live in the ground beneath the trees; fungus spores live on in dead leaves, curculio larvae in the cores of fallen fruit.

To go beyond this, gardeners might begin by spraying horticultural oils in winter and before green-tip (the first sign of unfurling leaf buds in early spring) to stifle pests before they hatch. For protection against the many fungus diseases, sulfur sprays, such as bordeaux mixture, are effective, especially if leaves are coated just before it rains. But one must beware of using them too often because too much sulfur will do damage to the soil life. Another fungus control that does not acidify the soil is to spray a tea made of equisetum leaves.

Organic insecticides, like Dipel (*Bacillus thuringiensis,* a disease of caterpillars), for instance, and rotenone (a plant derivative), can be added to the oil sprays or sprayed by themselves as needed. Peaceful Valley Farm Supply is a good source for all these materials. But this is territory that must be explored with the greatest caution. In living systems intervention always threatens disruption. The fact that an oil, organic fungicide, or insecticide is not inherently poisonous to humans is good news. But it may still cause harm by unbalancing the soil or by killing the many beneficial insects (on which healthy orchards depend) as well as harmful ones. This does not mean that one cannot intervene at all, only that one must do so with care and respect.

The organic care of fruit trees, still a developing art, is one of the subtlest, most entrancing forms of horticulture. The more gardeners strengthen their trees and avoid the conditions that bring about disease, the less they need resort to poison. The more they can learn about the life cycle of the buds and of insects, the more they can intervene in ways that help and do not also harm. A whole literature of calendars, schedules, and materials exists (the Bio-Dynamic Farming and Gardening Association is a good source for that information). Proper discussion of these methods would go far beyond the scope of this book. But applying them does not go beyond the scope of any gardener who feels stirred by their challenges.

Sheltering wild trees

Gardening with native trees might be the opposite extreme from the discipline of the home orchard. But while fruit trees evoke the sheltered gardens of the past, gardening with "wild" unimproved native trees may be a glimpse of the gardens of the future. I find I want both: the fruit trees because they speak of home and cultivation, and the wild trees—the same ones that grow just outside the

garden in woods and marshes and abandoned farm fields—
because they anchor my garden in its locality.

When a wild tree is given space, light, and loving attention, it
can grow into extraordinary beauty. The archetype of the tree is
made visible, and therefore also the place where the garden is.
Here on Long Island, red cedars follow the creeks in stately blue-
green processions, and stand in sociable groves wherever a field is
unmowed. Spring is announced by the pale flutter of light shadbush blossom. Without cedars and shadbush my garden could be
anywhere, but with them I know exactly where I live.

There is an ancient impulse in gardening to plant the world in
microcosm: to grow trees and flowers from every corner of the
globe in one tiny space. There will always be wonder
and paradox in doing this kind of gardening.
But these days, as wilderness is threatened,
another longing expresses itself. Where I live,
as all over the world, the wild places are vanishing and species of native trees are disap-
pearing because the sites where they like
to grow have been dug up and built on.
Almost the only places here where one can
see the eastern white cedar and the sweet bay magnolia—whose
scent wafts through summer air long after the spring-blooming
magnolias are over—are in gardens. Gardeners today often play a
new role, not of collecting the exotic and strange, but of keeping
the essence of a place alive, guarding the seeds of the future.

An inconspicuous source of joy in any garden is a small holding bed for trees. I use a corner of my vegetable garden. Because I
am not a very tidy weeder, I quite often find seedling white oaks

in my flower bed, and tiny hazel trees, and have even got American holly out of the wilder part of the "lawn." I dig them up and store them in that bed. I have no definite plans for this small forest; I might need some of it someday, or perhaps someone I know will. Meanwhile I watch it grow.

> Because you are
> only
> a seed,
> chestnut tree, autumn, earth,
> water, heights, silence
> prepared the germ,
> the floury density,
> the maternal eyelids
> that buried will again
> open towards the heights
> the simple majesty
> of foliage,
> the damp plan
> of new roots,
> the ancient but new dimensions
> of another chestnut tree in the earth.
>
> Pablo Neruda, from "Ode to a Chestnut on the Ground"

Chapter 12 Tools and Time

Spades take up leaves
No better than spoons,
And bags full of leaves
Are light as balloons.

I make a great noise
Of rustling all day
Like rabbit and deer
Running away.

But the mountains I raise
Elude my embrace,
Flowing over my arms
And into my face.

I may load and unload
Again and again
Till I fill the whole shed,
And what have I then?

Next to nothing for weight,
And since they grew duller
From contact with earth,
Next to nothing for color.

Next to nothing for use.
But a crop is a crop,
And who's to say where
The harvest shall stop?

Robert Frost, "Gathering Leaves"

234 – Bringing a Garden to Life

O
n the south bank of the Thames, opposite and a bit upriver from the Houses of Parliament, the fourteenth-century church of St. Mary's-in-Lambeth rocks a little with passing trucks and double-decker London buses. Twenty years ago, St. Mary's was scheduled to be razed for a parking lot, but was saved at the last moment and after long effort by a band of gardeners determined to honor the memory of the John Tradescants, father (1570–1638) and son (1608–1662), who lie buried in its tiny churchyard.

The Tradescants, gardeners to kings Charles I and II, were among the first global botanizers, traveling to Russia, Spain, North Africa, and the Near East (the father) and twice to the Virginia colony (the son). They were looking for the useful and beautiful, and brought back to England apricot trees, lilacs, yellow jasmine, asters, new apple varieties, red maples, spiderworts, and tulip trees. Around their small stone tomb with its worn epitaph ("Transplanted now themselves . . ."), only a wall away from the speeding cars and taxis, bees hover over specimens of more than a hundred different plants, all of them now intimately associated with English gardens but unknown there before those heroic journeys.

The modern gardeners who planted the churchyard garden also formed the Tradescant Trust and saved the church, reconsecrating it, not directly to God, but to gardening. The church is now the Museum of Garden History. Since the church was not very big, the museum is quite small. But though small it is lively, for the history it traces is not so much of gardens as of gardening—

the introduction of plants, the development of techniques and tools. A small case displays a set of four comfortable-looking round slippers designed to be worn by the horse that pulled the lawn mower, with the purpose of avoiding hoofprints on the grass.

Among the brass tablets set into a chapel wall is one so ancient it can barely be made out. It reads:

Cuthbert Turnstall
Born 1474 Died 1559
Bishop of London afterward Bishop of Durham
By Henry VIII deprived of the see by Edward VI committed to
the Tower 1551 and again in 1552 by Mary restored 1553
by Elizabeth again deprived 1559 he died under Bishop
Parten's roof and lies buried in the chancel of this
church.

Above the bones of this poor bishop, so unsettled in his life-time by the vicissitudes of politics, religious wars, and other people's ambitions, now stand glass cases containing a collection of early flowerpots, displays showing The History of the Watering Can and The History of the Spade. Not a great deal has changed from the Middle Ages to the present: beneath the rust one can observe that the spouts and blades of watering cans and spades have evolved only slowly over the past five hundred years, and, like the horse's slippers, their shapes describe both the job to be done and the creature who does it.

Not long ago I happened to be in London on some disturbing family business and took a rainy afternoon off to cross the river at low tide and become the lone visitor to the Museum of Garden History. I was reminded there of my own watering can and spade at home in Sag Harbor. My life, like the lives of so many these days and Bishop Cuthbert's then, has been blown about by outside events. But my tools have stayed the same: sensible, modest, just doing their job, practical and eternal.

A few good tools

The whole trick with tools is not to have too many, but to have just the right ones. By the right ones I mean tools that work and are worthy of a gardener's love. This is not too much to ask. Gardening tools evolved to suit the habits of humans and of plants and soil over thousands of years; by now they should be marvels of design, and they often are. A good tool is a pleasure to hold, well balanced in itself, not too heavy, not too light, sharp enough to connect decisively with the job, leaving behind clean edges, clear furrows. A tool like that cannot help being beautiful, and a gardener cannot contemplate it hanging on its peg or hook without wanting to take it down and get to work.

Good gardening tools are a little harder to find than shoddy ones that do not work well and fall apart easily. But if one looks carefully, some of the best tools can be found close to home. My favorite trowel, unbreakable with a solid shank, good heft, and an ash handle, is made in the United States by Union tools and it is still sold in my hardware store and probably many others. The sturdiest shovels and the best-designed hoes turn up leaning on the back walls of cellars and garages where they have been forgotten for a generation. Local yard sales are a prime source for gardeners willing to do a little sanding and sharpening. But often one has to look farther away.

Several mail-order catalogues sell beautiful, well-made tools; some reliable companies are listed in the Readings and Resources section at the back of the book. More and more one has to search for something as basic as a spade through page after page of plaster frogs and orange clogs, but the spades are still there. Gardeners willing to sift through the knickknacks, compare specifications and prices among four or five catalogues, and send things back if they are not comfortable to use (a tool, like a pair of shoes, has to fit), can ultimately find what they need.

Tools made carefully by small specialized companies have to be more expensive than the mass-produced items one finds in chain stores. But good tools last almost forever, becoming truly one's own, while a bad tool will quickly have to be thrown away. I still have most of the tools I started gardening with, and some were already old and well used when I got them. Good steel can be resharpened, wooden handles sanded down and oiled with a little linseed oil, or just one's own sweaty hands, till they are smooth as skin. A spade with a blade like a knife and a solid ash handle might cost twice as much as a chain-store one with an uncomfortable metal and plastic handle and a dull edge; but if gardeners can afford the outlay, it will save money in the end, and help them love the job and do it well.

To make a beginning, every gardener needs:

spade and digging fork Ideally these would be of matching size and weight, with comfortable D-shaped handles of a length to suit one's height. They are a gardener's chief companions and it is important that one like them.

two trowels One should be wide and capacious (like the Union trowel) with a strong handle, for planting bulbs and small plants. The other should be sharp and pointy—stainless steel is excellent—for moving seedlings without damaging their roots.

two hoes Both of these should have small, sharp heads for precision weeding, but one should be long-handled for hoeing standing up, and the other a hand hoe for sitting or kneeling at the job.

straight metal rake This is for preparing seedbeds.

hand pruners To make precise cuts, one really needs the parrot-beak type of pruner. I use Felco no. 6, the small hands model, even though my hands are quite big. Their blades are big and sharp enough to prune shrubs and young fruit trees, yet small enough to get close in to tiny rosebuds.

watering can A four-gallon can with a fine rose on its spout is indispensable for the gentle watering of seedlings, or for when one wants to just water a transplant or two without dragging a hose through the garden.

wheelbarrow Some people like two-wheeled carts, which are light and hold a lot. But the original one-wheeled design is still best for carrying heavy loads through narrow places, especially if it has comfortable handles and an inflatable tire.

A gardener might begin with these tools and not buy any more until he or she is sure their possibilities are exhausted. A sharp spade can do double duty as a knife for dividing perennials, also as an edger for keeping grass out of beds; with small pruners one might not need gardening scissors, and so on. Still, one usually does end up buying a few more tools, according to the direction the garden is taking.

If there are a lawn and trees one might need:

fan-shaped bamboo rakes For leaf-raking in fall and spring two
sizes are needed, one with about a fourteen-inch head for
the lawn, and a small one with a six-inch head for between
plants.

grass shears I recommend ones with long handles, for edging
beds that border the lawn.

lawn mower Gardeners might consider the kind one pushes, no
motor. This only works if one is willing to limit the size of
one's lawn to what one can comfortably mow with such a
machine. It can be worth it. This kind of mower always
starts, makes a pleasing sound that does not upset anyone,
and allows the gardener to think and to smell new-mown
grass while mowing.

For pruning branches up to four inches thick, the small red-
handled *Felco folding saw* is sharp and very good for working in
tight corners. A long-tined *pitchfork* and capacious *shovel* are useful for tossing compost and carrying in manure; but until I got a
pitchfork for Christmas three years ago, I managed with the spade
and digging fork. I still have not got a shovel, but I would like one.
Gardeners with rows of vegetables may want a *scuffle hoe*. Those
with a lot of brush might need a *machete*.

Shelter for tools and gardeners

There has to be a place to keep these tools, or they will be left out
in the rain or lost. In gardening, where so much depends on time-
liness, it is important to be able to find the right tool just when
one needs it. A good place for tools is on a rack of pegs and
broom holders, with a shelf beneath it for a couple of strong crates

or baskets in which to keep small hand tools and balls of string. The rack could be in a mudroom, or on an outside wall with a lean-to roof, or even in the living room, if that is where the garden door is. Good tools are nice to look at.

If, however, one can manage to have one, a garden shed is not only the most useful container of tools but may be a kind of tool in itself. In many communities, gardeners are allowed to put up a shed without a building permit since, with no foundation, it is considered a movable structure. Sheds can be bought in kit form from Agway and other companies. But a friend of mine with no previous building experience built his own eight-by-ten-by-eight-foot shingled hut from plans he bought at the lumberyard, using windows and a door he found at the dump. It took him about a month, working in his spare time, and he ended up with a plain, solid, but oddly beautiful little garden shed.

A garden shed need not spoil the view; it can even help to shape the garden, creating an extra edge or interesting corner. The space behind it might become a small garden within the garden; a bench against its wall makes a sheltered and secluded seat. Clematis, roses, or an espaliered tree can climb on the south wall. Or rafters might be extended outward to make a pergola on which to grow wisteria or grapes.

When we moved into our house there already was a small shed, inconspicuously aged into position at the edge of the garden about fifty feet from the house and under a maple tree. I think, from sinkers and shot I found, that it was originally meant for hunting gear and fishing tackle rather than hoes and rakes. But in size, construction, and ambience, it is the perfect garden shed. Made of cedar boards with a shingled roof, it sits a few inches off the ground on sturdy posts. Like my friend's homemade shed, it measures eight feet by ten feet in area, and it is nine feet tall at the ridge. Inside, its framing provides good hanging racks for the spade, fork, hoes, shears, and rakes. An old chest of drawers came with the shed, and there I keep seed packets, hose attachments, string. There is still enough floor space for watering cans, bags of lime and of grass seed, and even the lawn mower (another advantage of a push mower is that the shed in which one keeps it does not smell of gasoline).

The most important feature of our shed, and I would say of any shed, is a small window that allows light in and a view out (in our case the window faces east and the view is of gooseberry and currant bushes, sky and distant sea). The significance of a window is that it immediately makes the shed much more than a place to keep the spade out of the rain. A garden shed with a window and a chair is a sanctuary. Ours has no room for a table—what with the chest, lawn mower, watering cans, and so forth—but we did fit a workbench, made of two thick boards on brackets, directly under the window. After a year or two we went so far as to hook up a small woodstove and pipe.

I wrote my first book in that garden shed, holding the door

open with my foot when the woodstove burned too hot and closing it when the snow blew in. Ostensibly I moved there to escape my small children, who drew pictures on the manuscript. But actually there is no better place to quiet and enliven the mind than a small, uninsulated building through whose cracks the winds can still blow, and which is connected not to the telephone or electricity, but to the pulses of the garden.

Books as tools

On the shed wall, between the handles of the hoe and the rake, a small bookshelf is part of my tool collection. A gardener's imagination expands along with a knowledge of what is possible. I have been gradually building a collection of illustrated books with an A-to-Z approach, like *Perennials for American Gardens, The International Book of Trees, A Modern Herbal.* All these books have photographs or drawings of each plant they describe, and at least a paragraph on its habits and requirements. Such books allow me to identify the flowers, bushes, and trees that I see here and there and wonder if I could grow in my garden. They also introduce me to plants I may never have seen but will now look out for.

One of the reasons my shed is so pleasant is that there is no risk of coming across little bottles of poison in it. In their place is a copy of *The Organic Gardener's Handbook of Natural Insect and Disease Control* from the Rodale Press, which encourages gardeners not to study diseases but plants and their surroundings. Contemplative gardeners instinctively recoil from the quick and deadly approach to insects and disease. Poisons in the garden often kill many more kinds of creatures than they are meant to, sometimes endangering people too, and they cannot ultimately succeed if the causes of the problem are not addressed. But for an ecological approach to be more than a romantic notion, a gardener must be armed with specific information, and this the Rodale handbook lucidly provides.

The first section is an alphabetical guide to the common garden plants, each entry beginning with cultural requirements, then proceeding to a description of their characteristic ailments. To consult this book is to learn in the most direct way that almost all plant "diseases" are not alien visitations but the result of a plant's not getting what it needs. Perhaps it is struggling in the shade when it loves the sun or the other way around. Or it might be an acid-loving plant growing in a chalky soil, or its place is too wet, too dry, too crowded, or too exposed. Effective cures do not come out of bottles but through understanding and improving the situation, by moving the plant, keeping the garden clear of debris, enlivening the soil.

The insect-and-pest section is an encyclopedia in itself, with fascinating color photographs of every plant-eating pest a gardener is likely to meet (including slugs and snails) in each stage of their respective life cycles, and illustrations of the damage they do—very useful when, as often happens, the creature eats only at night. Also included, so that one leaves them alone, are photographs of the insects that pollinate the plants or that feed on the plant-eaters: the good wasps, the mantises, the bees. The text points out that about ninety percent of the insects in the garden are beneficial, and that resorting to insecticides, even "organic" ones, threatens the fine-tuned web of being on which the garden depends.

Knowing the life cycles and feeding habits of the pests can help a gardener steer clear of infestations, especially in the vegetable garden, where gardeners can sometimes time their plantings to avoid peak hatching times of hungry larvae. Though the Rodale book reluctantly offers the names of biological and mild chemical insecticides (boric acid, for instance, and ammonia) that might be used to deal with "emergencies," it makes it clear that for gardeners a much more effective approach is to direct one's efforts toward growing healthy balanced plants in a living soil. Gardeners quickly observe in their own gardens that the first plants to be attacked are those that are already weak, or past their prime, or sometimes those that come already over-fertilized from garden centers (aphids are drawn to rampant growth). Plants that are young and healthy will either be ignored, or if they are attacked, have a much better chance of surviving the onslaught. Thus the only real pest-and-disease control is good gardening practice.

PRACTICE AND PHILOSOPHY

This book has attempted to introduce gardeners to the rudiments of good practice—soil work and composting, planting, weeding, pruning. Once they begin, and especially if they find these activities interesting in themselves, gardeners will learn infinitely more just by gardening, year by year, and paying attention to what happens. Meanwhile, many gardeners may also want to have handy, for periodic consultation, one or two general reference books on plants and methods, the pages of which will soon become marked by earthy fingerprints, in the same way one's favorite cookbooks are stained with flour and oil.

I hesitate to say what those books will be. Each gardener will find his or her favorites. Dipping into the literature of gardening one soon discovers that even basic gardening books vary widely from one another in their fundamental approach to the craft. All will agree that the ground should not be worked when wet, nor roses pruned before a frost, but they will differ on many other matters. I think this is as it should be. Gardening is not only science but art, and not just law but lore. The differences arise from the authors' various experiences and, even more, out of their underlying views of what a garden is. To judge how far to follow an author's recommendations, a gardener needs to determine in what ways that author's vision resonates with her or his own.

For example, I have learned a great deal from Louise and James Bush-Brown's exhaustive *America's Garden Book,* first published in 1939, revised many times, and still in print. Time after time I have consulted its tables of suggested plants for different situations and of the times to divide perennials and prune various shrubs, and it has an honored place on my shed shelf. But from the moment I read, "It is disheartening to learn that in spite of all modern science has done, no insect species has ever been known to be completely exterminated," I knew I could not blindly follow all its instructions. (I am happy to report that this frightening sentence has been excised from the new edition, revised in 1996 by Howard S. Irwin and the Brooklyn Botanic Garden staff, and replaced with a much more insect-friendly approach.)

On the other hand Liberty Bailey's 1898 *Manual of Gardening,* for all its sometimes obsolete horse-drawn technology, inspired me with total confidence with these words:

> We are wont to covet the things that we cannot have: but we are happier when we love the things that grow because they must. A patch of lusty pigweeds, growing and crowding in

luxuriant abandon, may be better and a more worthy object of affection than a bed of coleus in which every spark of life and spirit and individuality has been sheared out and suppressed.

Because I believe that gardeners who love to garden do so precisely because of the "spark of spirit" that so often reveals itself there, igniting in turn the spirit of the gardener, I am drawn to those writers and teachers of gardening who acknowledge this relationship in their methods. Often it is those who have gone most deeply into their subject who do so. Bailey, who grew up on a Michigan orchard in the 1860s, wrote his manual out of his conviction that gardening civilizes not only plants, but people. He wrote a series of seven "background books," beginning with *The Holy Earth* and ending with *The Garden Lover,* addressing the relationship between nature and the soul. But he wrote these in his moments away from composing most of the fundamental textbooks of American horticulture, editing the *Standard Horticultural Cyclopedia,* and presiding as dean of the Cornell School of Agriculture.

The notion that the quiet contemplation of growing plants is an opportunity to know what cannot otherwise be known has informed many schools of gardening in the past. They are linked one to another by golden tendrils that lead also into the present and the future. The exquisite Taoist gardens of ancient China, described vividly in Osvald Siren's *Gardens of China* and preserved in the paintings of the Sung dynasty, were intended as revelations of the *chi* or life-spirit as it existed in a particular place; in a similar yet different way, so were the Buddhist gardens of Japan, whose character is expressed in the intensely focused verse of the great haiku poets. Basho wrote:

When the winter chrysanthemums go,
there's nothing to write about
but radishes.

and:

More than ever I want to see
in those blossoms at dawn
the god's face.

R. H. Blyth, a scholar and translator of Japanese haiku, wrote in a commentary that "though Goethe's understanding of science was to Basho unknown, he shares with him the knowledge that there is nothing behind phenomena, 'they are themselves the meaning.'" Basho lived in seventeenth-century Japan, Goethe in late-eighteenth-century Germany. Like Basho, Goethe found spirit in nature, not in any vague Romantic mood, but with absolute precision. Besides writing *Faust* and his uniquely beautiful lyric poetry, Goethe developed a scientific method of his own to challenge the new analytic methods of his time. He made systematic studies of living plants (often those in his own garden, where he sketched the seeds of calendulas, the flowering of the perfoliate rose) as they grow and change. On his travels he observed how the same plant in different places takes on different forms yet retains a distinct unchanging archetype beneath all change. The results of these observations are expressed in the remarkable essay *The Metamorphosis of Plants,* short enough to fit neatly onto any toolshed shelf. How, Goethe asked, can anything be learned of life through the study of what is dead? To know the sources of life one must observe it as it lives, in motion and change.

BIODYNAMICS

In this century the Goethean approach was continued and developed by Rudolf Steiner (editor of the Goethe scientific archive) who brought meditative and practical techniques of horticulture together in the methodology known as biodynamics, which has been mentioned several times in these gardening hints. Gardeners who are drawn to the contemplative aspect of gardening may find both sound garden advice and inspiration in books by the various authors who follow this approach.

Although there are biodynamic methods that are of specific concern to gardeners, the original impulse behind biodynamics did not directly concern gardening, but was an attempt to deal with a crisis in farming and planetary ecology. Invited to lecture to a group of farmers who were concerned, already in 1924, with poor crop yields and loss of vitality in seeds, Steiner presented an approach to farming based not on analysis of substances and estimated yields per pound of fertilizer, but on the apprehension of the living forces at work on and in plants. He said that in working with living systems all influences must be taken into account, from the particular nature of the animals that drop the manure, to minute trace quantities of elements in the soil, to the movements of the solar system. With the development of such understanding, he suggested, human consciousness working with plants and soil could lead not to an exploitation of the earth but to an enlivening of it. As this century of ecological foreboding draws to a close, the idea that human activity might actually make a positive contribution to nature comes to some people as a profound relief.

The recommendations that Steiner made were practical. He proposed establishing the farm as a self-sustaining organism, with particular methods of composting and soil treatment to ensure the production of wholesome food; he discussed the feeding of farm animals, the care of fruit trees. But the observations of nature on which his practical directives were based are subtle and difficult: some, one recognizes at once, wondering why one never noticed before; others are far more recondite. Steiner urged that all his suggestions be not only systematically tested, but developed further, and this continues to be done in field tests and laboratories. But it is clear that to actually work creatively with biodynamics—not just to follow given instructions—growers need to go beyond everyday perception and look deeply and meditatively into nature.

The circumstances of my life have brought me to visit many biodynamic farms, beginning twenty-one years ago with an apple orchard in Australia where I helped spray horn manure under heavy-branched Granny Smith and Gravenstein trees while small red and blue parrots swooped through the air. Biodynamic farms often feel like paradise gardens. To be "discrete organisms" they have to be diverse, so there are pastures as well as field crops, trees as well as meadows, ponds, herbs, and beehives. Like gardens, they are conceived as single harmonized entities. The hay smells sweet, the vegetables are tasty and idiosyncratic, with the most potatoish potatoes, the most carroty carrots. Birds sing in hedgerows and the cows—always with their horns intact—contentedly chew their cud.

Perhaps because to create them their farmers needed to employ the attentiveness to detail, the freshness of feeling and perception that usually belongs only to childhood, the farms I visited had the intensity of presence that evokes earliest memory:

... when meadow, grove, and stream,
The earth, and every common sight,
To me did seem
Apparelled in celestial light.

Although biodynamic farms are known around the world as among the most productive and sophisticated of the organic movement, their methods disturb conventional agronomists because of what is often described as the "contradiction" between their practical results and their origin in a spiritual view of the world. But gardeners who love to garden tend not to see any such contradiction. Gardens have always been windows on the unity of spirit and matter. So biodynamic gardening has developed alongside farming, and the gardens that result, while they do not resemble one another, also share a sweet intensity—though in them grow lilies, roses, honeysuckle, and doves, rather than grain, potatoes, and chickens.

Few gardeners read Steiner's original *Agriculture* lectures from which the method sprang, because the lectures were for farmers and because they have the reputation of being difficult (they are, but they are also quite wonderful, at once earthy and challenging to the imagination, poetic and full of humor). Gardeners are more likely to begin with one or several how-to books specifically for gardeners. John Soper's clear and straightforward *Bio-Dynamic Gardening* is on my shelf of essentials. It was written for English conditions, and it combines well with the *Pfeiffer Garden Book,* edited by Alice Heckel and written for American gardeners, which is especially useful for vegetables and herbs. There is an active Bio-Dynamic Farming and Gardening Association in this country that holds conferences and publishes a long list of books and pamphlets, offering very specific directions on constructing a compost heap, companion planting, making fruit-tree sprays, as well as on "the active perception of nature." In the end the best introduction to biodynamics is to try some part of it out.

Many of the loveliest gardens I have seen, full of life, beauty, and revelation, have been made by gardeners who have never heard of biodynamics. They have, however, all been made with love, attention, and awareness of place and time. I mention biodynamics because it is the only methodology I know that actively evokes such apprehensions, and as such it can be an important tool.

Time and the garden

The final tool on this list is a garden calendar. This is not bought, but made by oneself—a new one for each year, or a strong, thick one that can go on and on. It should probably be a blank notebook rather than a dated diary (so one can mark dates as they come), because on some days nothing will be written, while other days may take up many pages. The purpose of this calendar is to observe the connections that mark the passage of time.

Outside the garden, days of twenty-four hours or months of thirty-one days can be stretched or contracted like elastic bands to accommodate particular projects and adventures. Often it makes no difference if it is raining or sunny, day or night, spring or summer; the activity with which one is engaged follows its own independent trajectory. But in the garden, things happen quite differently. Time in the garden is inextricably linked to a thousand interrelated phenomena.

An ancient Long Island gardener, seeing me hesitate about taking my tomato plants outside, intoned, "If you're waiting for the last frost, wait till the peepers have stopped three times" (peepers being the tiny frogs that sing around the ponds on the first warm spring nights and stop again when the temperature dips). When I asked what would happen if I missed a night of no peeping and lost count, he said, "Wait until the barn swallows are back. Don't plant corn till the white oak bud is as long as a squirrel's ear. And don't plant peas till the beach peas are up."

Around here, potato farmers traditionally coincided their first plantings with the running of alewives (a small silver fish that travels in large shoals) out of the creeks and into the bay, and, in turn, the alewives time their run with the full moon nearest the vernal equinox. Today the Suffolk County Agricultural Extension Service tells the descendants of those farmers to watch for daylilies beginning to bloom by the roadside, so as to know when the third generation of potato bugs is out (so they can be destroyed forthwith), since apparently the lilies and the beetles need the same number of degree days to spring into action.

Gardeners respond to oak buds, alewives, beach peas flowering on the dunes, the greening of the brown grass—whatever indicators they have been told about, or have discovered for themselves to be reliable. Meanwhile the oak buds and alewives are responding to cosmic nudges the gardeners cannot see. Some of it is weather, fickle and unpredictable and moved in turn by nameless planetary tides, and now, it seems, by our own unknowing intervention. The rate at which lilac buds fatten varies a great deal from year to year according to the temperature of soil and air. To know about a particular year's weather, it is sensible to look at a lilac, a plant that is seldom fooled. But weather is not all: other plants are less susceptible to temperature and steadfastly follow agendas linked to the increasing and decreasing hours of light, the changing position of the sun in the sky, regardless of untimely frosts or thaws.

The effects on plant growth not only of the sun's annual journey and its dramatic effects but of the more subtle effects of the moon's monthly orbits through the celestial sphere were an object of serious study from ancient times through the Middle Ages and the Renaissance. For a few hundred years the subject was relegated to old wives; now that old wives are not so easily disparaged, their knowledge is being reappraised by conventional science, by organic and biodynamic farmers, and by gardeners who pay attention to what happens. *Stella Natura,* edited by Sherry Wildfeuer at Kimberton Hills Camphill Village, is a calendar published each year for farmers and gardeners, giving daily data on the position of the moon in relation to the constellations (astronomical, not astrological), perigee and apogee, eclipses, occultations, conjunctions, and more. Introductory essays offer explanations of these terms in clear reviews of basic astronomy, outlines of research on the effects on different types of plants and plant-work in relation to moon and planet position, and "encouragement to look up" in the form of a clear star chart to help gardeners see for themselves.

I tried for some years to use the *Stella Natura* as my gardening calendar. It did not work because the space in which to write one's own notes was never big enough to include the significant happenings that coincided with the planetary events: "April 20: Still cold, but sunny. Black-Seeded Simpson lettuce up, pear tree buds showing green. Queen Victoria rose looks dead. First osprey ate large fish on high branch of oak by shed." Instead, I began making my own calendars with day and date, transcribing the star facts off *Stella Natura* so they could be superimposed over the opening pear leaves, the perhaps dead rose, the osprey's return, in order that any relatedness would eventually reveal itself.

Homemade garden calendars belong on the shelf with the other reference books where they can be consulted in search of patterns of recurrence, spirals of growth, and variables of change. At first they provoke more questions than answers, but if one can reserve judgment, gradually pictures begin to form and the rhythms of the garden make themselves known, lucid and alive. Some gardeners may not want to bother with a notebook, preferring to trust those same observations to settle and collect in memory. Either way, awareness grows of the garden's intertwinedness with all that exists, including, of course, the gardener's own life, shaped by, at the same time as it shapes, the garden.

Readings
and Resources

The following is a list of suggested readings and of sources for plants, tools, associations, and materials, tied to the content of each chapter. It is by no means a comprehensive list, but it is tried and true. The books that are marked with an asterisk are not currently in print. I have listed them anyway because they are worth the trouble of finding. Public libraries may have them, and good horticultural collections certainly will; they frequently turn up in secondhand book stores. I hope that some will even be brought back into print.

Introduction

BOOKS

Hill, Lewis. *Cold Climate Gardening: How to Extend Your Growing Season by at Least 30 Days.* Pownall, Vt.: Storey Publishing, 1987.

Ladendorf, Sandra F. *Successful Southern Gardening: A Practical Guide for Year-Round Beauty.* Chapel Hill: University of North Carolina Press, 1989.

Sunset Western Garden Book. Menlo Park, Calif.: Sunset Books, 1988.

Vick, Roger. *Gardening: Plains and Upper Midwest.* Golden, Colo.: Fulcrum Publishing, 1991.

Chapter 1: *Making a Place*

BOOKS

Alexander, Christopher, et al. *A Pattern Language.* New York: Oxford University Press, 1977. This book is not directly about gardens, but it offers a unique way of learning to experience, and to consider analytically, what it is that makes a good place.

Eck, Joe. *Elements of Garden Design.* New York: Henry Holt, 1997. A well-written primer on the structural elements that make up a garden, allowing gardeners to think about them without feeling dictated to.

Klingborn, Arne. *The Ever Changing Garden.* Wynstones, Gloucestershire: The Lanthorn Press, 1988. Illustrations in watercolor and short essays beautifully illuminate the ways various cultures have perceived the garden from prehistory to the present day.

*Siren, Osvald. *Gardens of China.* New York: The Roland Press, 1948. A scholarly and poetic exposition of the history of Chinese gardens and their relation to Chinese poetry, painting, philosophy, and life.

Chapter 2: *Preparing the Ground*

BOOKS

Gershuny, Grace. *Start with the Soil.* Emmaus, Pa.: Rodale Press, 1993. Clear and comprehensive, full of helpful information about understanding and improving one's own garden soil.

PRODUCTS

Josephine Porter Institute for Applied Bio-Dynamics. P.O. Box 133, Woolwine, VA 24185. (540) 930-2463. The source for the horn manure spray as well as other biodynamic preparations, either individually or by annual subscription (with a newsletter).

Peaceful Valley Farm Supply. P.O. Box 2209, Grass Valley, CA 95945. (916) 272-4769. Mail-order organic soil amendments, cover crop seeds, good digging tools. Also offers a soil-testing service tied to organic amendments.

Snow Pond Farm Supply. R.R. 2, Box 1009, Belgrade, ME 04917. (800) 768-9998. Similar products to Peaceful Valley's, but based on the East Coast.

Chapter 3: *Compost*

BOOKS

Campbell, Stu. *Let It Rot: The Gardener's Guide to Composting.* Pownall, Vt.: Storey Publishing, 1990. Lively descriptions of a wide range of composting techniques; cheerful hints on what can go wrong and how to fix it.

Corrin, George. *Handbook on Composting and the Bio-dynamic Preparations.* Clent, England: Bio-Dynamic Agriculture Association, 1995. Thirty concisely written pages on making a serious compost pile; also a good introduction to using biodynamic preparations.

PRODUCTS

Johnny's Selected Seeds. Foss Hill Road, Albion, ME 04910. (207) 437-9244. Catalogue includes a well-designed cedar compost frame.

Josephine Porter Institute for Applied Bio-Dynamics (see notes to chapter 2) is the source for Pfeiffer compost starter and the biodynamic compost preparations.

Peaceful Valley Farm Supply and Snow Pond Farm Supply (see notes to chapter 2) for extra compost ingredients and equipment, and good literature.

Chapter 4: *Beginning from Seed*

BOOKS

Ashworth, Suzanne. *Seed to Seed: Seed Saving Techniques for the Vegetable Gardener.* Decorah, Iowa: Seed-Savers Exchange, 1995.

Bubel, Nancy. *The New Seed-Starters Handbook.* Emmaus, Pa.: Rodale Press, 1988. Clear, detailed information on seed-starting, plant by plant. Full of practical tips.

Johnston, Robert, Jr. *Growing Garden Seeds.* Booklet available from Johnny's Selected Seeds (see notes to chapter 3). A good introduction to saving and using your own seeds.

SEED CATALOGUES

Fedco Seeds. P.O. Box 520, Waterville, ME 04903. (207) 873-7333. Vegetables, flowers, herbs, cover crops, literature. An emphasis on seeds for northern climates.

J. L. Hudson, Seedsman. P.O. Box 1058, Redwood City, CA 94064. For gardeners interested in the baobab tree; the place to go for what cannot be found elsewhere.

Johnny's Selected Seeds (see notes to chapter 3). Johnny's was a pioneer in developing seeds suitable for organic gardeners—not all of their seeds are organic, but all varieties have been selected for growing without chemical fertilizers and pesticides. Many vegetable varieties, herbs, flowers, and now an interesting selection of medicinal herbs. Some good tools and books. A lot of helpful information in a beautifully organized catalogue.

Seeds of Change. P.O. Box 15700, Santa Fe, NM 87506. (505) 438-8080. All organically grown seeds—vegetables, flowers, herbs. Specializes in open-pollinated "heritage" varieties, many from Native American sources; the best beans, corn, and squash. Another source for biodynamic preparations.

Southern Exposure Seed Exchange. P.O. Box 170, Earlysville, VA 22936. (804) 973-4703. Specializes in seeds for warm climates.

Thompson and Morgan Inc. P.O. Box 1308, Jackson, NJ 08527.(800) 274-7333. A large selection of flowers, often rare and exciting, but many varieties are not for beginners.

Threshold Seeds. P.O. Box 701, Claverack, NY 12513. (518) 672-5509. Biodynamic farmers all across the country choose one or two of their best varieties to grow for seed and send them to Threshold Seeds. This catalogue is mostly a seed exchange for them, but whatever is left is sold to home gardeners. An interesting selection of open-pollinated vegetables, herbs, and a few flowers. High-quality biodynamic seeds, and a worthwhile endeavor to support.

ASSOCIATIONS

The Seed-Savers Exchange. 3076 N. Winn Road, Decorah, IA 52101. (319) 382-5990. A network of enthusiastic gardeners and plant lovers who are collecting and distributing seeds of rare varieties of food plants (the Flower and Herb Exchange—same address—does the same for herbs and flowers). Send $1.00 for brochure and membership information.

Chapter 5: *Transplanting and Propagating*

BOOKS

Brickell, Christopher, ed. *The Encyclopedia of Gardening Techniques.* New York: Exeter Books, Simon and Schuster, 1984. (Originally published in England as the Royal Horticultural Society's *Book of Gardening Techniques.*) Wonderfully clear diagrams and concise instruction on all kinds of transplanting and propagating techniques.

Chapter 6: *Weeding*

BOOKS

Agricultural Research Service of the United States Department of Agriculture. *Common Weeds of the United States.* Mineola, N.Y.: Dover Press, 1971. The best weed identification book. Line drawings, botanical description, range maps.

Pfeiffer, Ehrenfried E. *Weeds and What They Tell.* Kimberton, Pa.: Bio-Dynamic Farming and Gardening Association, 1990. (First published in 1950.)

Chapter 7: *Pruning*

BOOKS

*Bailey, Liberty Hyde. *The Pruning Book.* New York: Macmillan, Rural Science Series, 1912. Mostly about fruit trees, but Bailey's intro-

duction on the principles of all pruning is the clearest presentation
I have ever seen.

Bush-Brown, Louise and James. *America's Garden Book*. Revised by
Howard S. Irwin and Brooklyn Botanic Garden. New York: Macmillan, 1996. This is a good source for specific information on
when to prune what (as well as an excellent all-purpose garden
reference book).

Jekyll, Gertrude, and Mawley, Edward. Introduced and revised by Gra-
ham Stuart Thomas. *Roses for English Gardens*. New York: Penguin
Books, 1983. (First published in 1901.)

Joyce, David, and Brickell, Christopher. *The Complete Guide to Pruning
and Training Plants*. New York: Simon and Schuster, 1992. A beautifully illustrated and lucidly explained comprehensive guide.

TOOLS

A. M. Leonard, Inc. 241 Fox Drive, P.O. Box 816, Piqua, OH 45356. (800)
543-8955. A full line of high-quality, reasonably priced pruning
saws and hand clippers (also other good gardening tools).

Chapter 8: *Flowers*

BOOKS

Clausen, Ruth Rogers, and Ekstrom, Nicholas. *Perennials for American
Gardens*. New York: Random House, 1989. Alphabetically organized; clear photographs; comprehensive introduction to names
and habits of many well-known and less-known varieties of
perennials.

Jekyll, Gertrude. *Wood and Garden*. Woodbridge, England: Antique Col-
lectors Club, Baron Publishing, 1981. (First published in 1899.)
The great innovator of modern garden design was also a superb,
engaging writer. This book takes readers month by month
through her own garden. Although many of the plants mentioned

are not hardy in American gardens, the book is worth reading for pure inspiration—especially the chapter called "Colour in the Garden," which will infuse gardeners with Jekyll's love of plants and the impulse to see more in a flower bed than they might have thought possible.

Scaniello, Steven. *A Year of Roses*. New York: Henry Holt, 1997. Covers all aspects of growing roses with enthusiasm and without fear.

Taylor's Guide to Annuals. Boston: Houghton Mifflin Company, 1997. Organized by color; helps gardeners identify annuals; good hints on requirements and culture.

PLANTS AND BULBS

Dutch Gardens. P.O. Box 200, Adelphia, NJ 07710. (800) 818-3861. A wide selection of spring and summer bulbs from Holland, reasonably priced.

White Flower Farm. P.O. Box 50, Litchfield, CT 06759. (800) 503-9624. Perennials and bulbs by mail; plants carefully shipped. Almost a plant book in itself, this richly illustrated catalogue offers cultural requirements for each plant offered and describes and supplies many varieties.

Chapter 9: *Vegetables*

BOOKS

Heckel, Alice, ed. *The Pfeiffer Garden Book*. Kimberton, Pa.: The Bio-Dynamic Farming and Gardening Association, 1969. All aspects of vegetable gardening.

Jeavons, John. *How to Grow More Vegetables*. Berkeley, Calif.: Ten Speed Press, 1979. Emphasizes raised beds, a lot of good information on plant spacing and companion planting.

Philbrick, Helen and Gregg, Richard B. *Companion Plants and How to*

Use Them. Greenwich, Conn: Devin-Adair Company, 1975.
See notes to chapter 4 for vegetable seed sources.

Chapter 10: *Herbs*

BOOKS

Grieve, Maud. *A Modern Herbal*. Volumes I and II. Mineola, N.Y.: Dover
  Press, 1971.

Hylton, William, ed. *The Rodale Herb Book*. Emmaus, Pa.: Rodale Press,
  1974. Good section on cultivation and storage; also interesting
  non-gardening information on uses: in remedies, cooking, per-
  fumes, dyes.

SEEDS

Meadowbrook Herb Garden. 93 Kingstown Road, Wyoming, RI 02898.
  (401) 539-7603.

Chapter 11: *Trees in the Garden*

BOOKS

*Johnson, Hugh. *The International Book of Trees*. New York: Bonanza
  Books, Crown Publishers, 1980. Magnificent photographs of all
  the tree families, in gardens and around the world. Concise, well-
  written chapters on history and cultivation. Growth and hardiness
  charts.

The Peterson Field Guide Series. *A Field Guide to Trees and Shrubs*.
  Boston: Houghton Mifflin, 1972.

NURSERIES

Forestfarm. 990 Tetherow Road, Williams, OR 97544. (503) 846-7269.
  Large selection of very interesting trees and shrubs; young plants
  shipped in tubes for a few dollars per tree.

The following nurseries specialize in antique and modern pest-resistant fruit varieties appropriate to their own climatic conditions; gardeners should pick the one closest to their own.

Fedco Trees. P.O. Box 520, Waterville, ME 04903. fax:(207) 426-9005.
Rocky Meadow Orchard and Nursery. 360 Rocky Meadow Road N.W., New Salisbury, IN 47161. (812) 347-2213.
Sonoma Antique Apple Nursery. 4395 Westside Road, Healdsburg, CA 95448. (707) 433-6420.
Southmeadow Fruit Gardens. 10603 Cleveland Avenue, Baroda, MI 49101. (616) 469-2865. Will do custom grafting; also sells rootstocks for those interested in trying their hand.

ASSOCIATIONS
North American Fruit Explorers. R.R.1, Box 94, Chapin, IL 62628.

Chapter 12: *Tools and Time*

BOOKS
*Bailey, Liberty Hyde. *Manual of Gardening.* New York: Macmillan, 1912.
Bush-Brown, Louise and James. *America's Garden Book* (see notes to chapter 7).
Ellis, Barbara W., and Bradley, Fern. *The Organic Gardener's Handbook of Natural Insect and Disease Control.* Emmaus, Pa.: Rodale Press, 1992.
Goethe, Johann Wolfgang von. *The Metamorphosis of Plants.* Kimberton, Pa.: Bio-Dynamic Farming and Gardening Association, 1993.
Soper, John. *Bio-Dynamic Gardening.* Clent, England: Bio-Dynamic Agricultural Association, 1983.
Steiner, Rudolf. *Agriculture.* Kimberton, Pa.: Bio-Dynamic Farming and Gardening Association, 1993.
Wildfeuer, Sherry, ed. *Stella Natura.* Kimberton, Pa.: Bio-Dynamic Farming and Gardening Association, 1997.

ASSOCIATIONS

Bio-Dynamic Farming and Gardening Association, P.O. Box 550, Kimberton, PA 19942. (610) 935-7797. An active organization with conferences, regional groups, and newsletter. A catalogue of books and even farm produce.

TOOLS

A. M. Leonard, Inc. See notes to chapter 7.

Gardener's Supply Company. 128 Intervale Road, Burlington, VT 05401. (800) 444-6417. The best hoes and many practical gadgets.

Smith and Hawken. P.O. Box 6900, Florence, KY 41022. (800) 776-3336. High-quality English spades and forks, trowels, and the Japanese hand hoe.

Walt Nicke Company. P.O. Box 433, Topsfield, MA 01938. (508) 887-3388. Some rare treasures, including the best trombone sprayer.

Acknowledgments

For my own gardener's education, I must first thank my mother, Janne Rey, who led me into the garden through the atmosphere of absorbed contentment that surrounded her whenever she worked there. Hugh Williams taught me much of what I know, both the technique and the seriousness of it all, and always said the garden was beautiful, no matter what was in it. The Bio-Dynamic Association conferences I attended in Spring Valley, New York in the 1970s (in particular lectures by Herbert Koepf, Heinz Grotzke, and David Schwartz) permanently broadened my point of view. And Joel Morrow's penetrating, practical, and poetic essays on growing vegetables (which appeared in the journal "Bio-dynamics" from 1984 to 1992) were my lessons in how much can be noticed.

Michael Katz asked, "When are you going to write a book?" He is my agent and truly defines the word: every conversation with him leaves me with a clearer mind and sharper purpose. Without Toni Burbank, my editor at Bantam Books, this book would not have been written. She saw a tiny seed and envisioned the whole plant: I am deeply grateful. Sally Booth, Kathleen Ebin, Karl Grossman, and Jane Hirshfield read the manuscript at different crucial stages and helped me along, each in their own essential way. Then David Bullen designed the book with thoughtfulness, clarity, and grace.

On more days than I can count, Roisin Bateman, Sally Booth, Deborah Enright, and Christopher Tekverk included my youngest child into their families while I worked, allowing me to write this book with undivided attention because I knew that she was flourishing. This is the most liberating gift a writer who is also a mother can receive. There is no way to properly thank them, except perhaps to hope that the community of work and loving friendship that we and our children share is a blueprint for the truly extended family of the future.

Permissions

Index

About the Author

Carol Williams has written about architecture, art, and horticulture. A graduate of M.I.T., she has lived in Sag Harbor since 1974 and consults on gardening.

A Note on the Illustrations

The drawings of garden presences that illuminate this book were taken from the personal notebooks of the English painter Newton Haydn Stubbing (1921–1983), who lived the last ten years of his life on the East End of Long Island. His paintings—explorations of light and atmosphere based on the intense observation of nature—may be seen in the permanent collection of the Tate Gallery in London and at the Cathedral of St. John the Divine in New York City. The author wishes to thank Yvonne Hagen Stubbing for her great kindness in allowing the use of his sketches in this book.